The

I0149572

Year

of the

Poet IV

November 2017

The Poetry Posse

inner child press, ltd.

The Poetry Posse 2017

Gail Weston Shazor

Shareef Abdur Rasheed

Albert Carrasco

Teresa E. Gallion

hülya n. yılmaz

Kimberly Burnham

Elizabeth Castillo

Jackie Davis Allen

Joe DaVerbal Minddancer

Jen Walls

Nizar Sartawi

Caroline 'Ceri' Nazareno

Bismay Mohanty

Faleeha Hassan

Anna Jakubczak Vel RattyAdalan

William S. Peters, Sr.

General Information

The Year of the Poet IV
November 2017 Edition

The Poetry Posse

1st Edition : 2017

Publisher Information

1st Edition : Inner Child Press
intouch@innerchildpress.com
www.innerchildpress.com

ISBN-13 : 978-1970020304 (inner child press, ltd.)

ISBN-10 : 197002030X

$ 12.99

WHAT WOULD LIFE BE WITHOUT A LITTLE POETRY?

Dedication

This Book is dedicated to

Janet P. Caldwell

&

Alan W. Jankowski

Poetry . . .

The Poetry Posse

past, present & future

our Patrons and Readers

the Spirit of our Everlasting Muse

&

the Power of the Pen

to effectuate change!

In the darkness of my life
I heard the music
I danced . . .
and the Light appeared
and I dance

Janet P. Caldwell

Janet Perkins Caldwell

Rest In Peace

February 14, 1959 ~ September 20, 2016

Rest In Peace Dear Brother

Alan W. Jankowski

16 March 1961 ~ 10 March 2017

Poets . . .
sowing seeds in the
Conscious Garden of Life,
that those who have yet to come
may enjoy the Flowers.

Foreword

Feelings need poets to get their portraits painted. Besides every work of poetry, transports the reader into an alternate realm, where imagination turns into reality and the insane becomes the do-able.

There's this poem, "The Voice of the Rain", the poem explains water cycle in the most creative way possible and it's a matter of utmost stupefaction that the poetry accounts for such process in the nature which wasn't discovered until later by the scientists.

In a way, poets give a way to mankind to comprehend even on the most unbelievable fantasies. They direct minds and I believe that literature is the most logical of all subjects.
Poems enables us to see things in ways they have never seen before. And the poet's job, you see, is not to give us straight, encyclopaedic fact but to tell us something new or to tell us something old in a new way- to give us fresh images.

In this issue of YOTP, the theme lies 'Thanksgiving'. What can be more beautiful than thanking poets and their children -poetry, which helps this world shape from beautiful manifestation into a heavenly reality. May the light of education keep on lighting stronger every single day and minds be delighted by the magic of verses.

Bismay Mohanty

Preface

Dear Family and Friends,

Our theme for this month of November is Thankfulness and Gratitude.

i Offered Thanks

I awakened this morning, and i offered a prayer of gratitude to the Progenitor of my life, . . . my God.

There are many things to be thankful for. They can be found in the Good and that which is perceived as Evil, the Light and the Dark.

I offered thanks for all the Woe in my life, for through it i learned that i had the gift of Endurance and Temperance.

I offered thanks for all those who have left my life through Death, Moving Away, Growing Up and the ending of Relationships, for it has taught me to appreciate those who are in my life NOW, as well as how to truly cherish the memories of the blessings of their presence i once enjoyed.

I offered thanks for all the Dark Days ... yes, for the dark days brought to me an understanding of how i could truly employ, not only the light of those found in the not so dark days, but how to utilize to the best of my own abilities, and that small light of my own that resides within me.

I offered thanks for all the Anger i suffered through . . . that of my own and that of others. Through my anger i have come to know the true meaning of humility. This gift was imparted to me in being chastised and scolded by others, and in having to be the one who must later apologize for their errancies of character, attitude and expression.

I offered thanks for all the times when i was down on my luck. It was, and is those times i realize that luck and being down, was my own choosing, and that i had the power to alter my perspectives of how i viewed my life. Should i go forth with disdain for the hand that life has dealt me or should i cling to such powerful forces of hope and faith? These powers do have a transformative ability to change my energy to something magnificent and grand.

I offered thanks for all the Tears i have cried . . . for whatever reasons. Tears truly have a deep cleansing ability to alleviate my soul of the angst i have collected through many of life's circumstances.

I offered thanks for all the "NOs" i have heard, given me by life when i so wanted to hear a "Yes". Yes, in reflection, many times those "Yes's" i wished for would have been detrimental to my higher good. I did not always understand this, nor did i care at that moment, for i was blinded by my own "Self Oriented" desires and my finite and limited perspectives on the whole of what may "Be" or "Become". I have grown tremendously because of each and every one of those "NOs" . . . and again i must say . . . I am Thankful.

As you read this, you may say to your self, to be thankful is a good thing . . .or not. But to be thankful, i have found to be personally empowering on so many "Life Levels". It has added unto my abilities to make it through many other circumstances i could not have navigated early on in my life. It was all the setbacks that taught me how to garner my fortitude to press on. It is all those disappointments that taught me Tolerance, Acceptance and Patience. It has taught me some wonderful things about my own abilities.

This does not mean that i did not want things . . . i did, and i do! This does not mean i gave up on life . . . NO . . i live to the fullest i can . . .when i remember who i am and have the mind-set to do so. Simply put, through the Storms "Life" has so mercifully sent my way, i have come realize a greater expanse of my own abilities. I have come to know the meaning of peace found in the "Eye of the Storm". I have discovered that i am so much more than i believed and so much more than what i have been *Taught* and *Told* . . . as are you!

The biggest and most profound aspect of my existence i have come to reckon with is that there is a Power we have . . . yes "WE", that is connected to some force we have yet to fully comprehend. Most of us about this wonderful plane of existence identify this as God. Whether you are a believer or not, matters not much, for even Science cannot deny this immeasurable force that connects us all to a "One" reality, whether we identify it as Evolution or Creation. They are but words, as are these! But, what is real in this seemingly temporal existence of ours is what we feel. I pray that you take the time to "feel" the goodness of who you are and teach and show others through your example as well to embrace, not just their possibilities of what they may become, but the grand aspects of what we already ARE . . . Right Now . . . Right Here !

Finally, I offered thanks for all the Love i have had in my life and that which still resides, which is "ALL LOVE". The love that appears to have went away, left the Gift of Experience and thus a Lesson or two behind. And, funny thing, these lessons are still mine, the Lesson and the Love.

The Love i have today . . . it is filled with possibilities of what it may become. Who can contain such energy with a closed hand or closed heart . . . . None !!!! Love seems to be that Universal Language that is now awakening and calling to all Souls to "Allow" the opening of our Heart's Door . . . Do you hear the knocking ?

I have offered thanks this day for you. I Awakened this Morning . . .

So in conclusion, take the time, read what we have to offer, and enjoy the journey.

Building Cultural Bridges

Bless Up

Bill

PS

Do Not forget about the World Healing, World Peace Poetry effort.

**For Free Downloads of Previous Issues of
The Year of the Poet**

www.innerchildpress.com/the-year-of-the-poet

T able of C ontents

T he P oetry P osse

Table of Contents . . . *continued*

November Features   111

Inner Child News   141

Other Anthological Works   151

Poets, Writers . . . know that we are the enchanting magicians that nourishes the seeds of dreams and thoughts . . . it is our words that entice the hearts and minds of others to believe there is something grand about the possibilities that life has to offer and our words tease it forth into action . . . for you are the Poet, the Writer to whom the Gift of Words has been entrusted . . .

~ wsp

poetry is . . .

The Tree of Life
Thankfulness and Gratitude

This month of November, i decided to do something a bit different. Our theme this month was Thankfulness and Gratitude, so i decided to take this opportunity to create a different perspective on our Tree of the Month. At first i was going to name it The Thanksgiving Tree", but i quickly realized how offensive this term is to our Native American brothers and sisters. So, i decided to name the Tree, *The Tree of Life.* For myself, life is always at its best expression when i walk, think, breathe from a position of Gratitude and Thankfulness.

Though there is not a thing wrong with being grateful and giving thanks, many of us do not appreciate the gravity of such actions. We can make a difference in our lives, the lives of others who are here with us, and those of our past, and thereby effectuate the change we desire for the generations to come.

So in conclusion let us celebrate our abilities to appreciate life and pay this loving sentiment and blessing forward.

Bless Up

Bill

The

Year

of the

Poet III

November 2017

The Poetry Posse

inner child press, ltd.

Poetry succeeds where instruction fails.

~ wsp

Gail

Weston

Shazor

This is a creative promise ~ my pen will speak to and for the world. Enamored with letters and respectful of their power, I have been writing for most of my life. A mother, daughter, sister and grandmother I give what I have been given, greatfilledly.

Author of . . .

"An Overstanding of an Imperfect Love"
&
Notes from the Blue Roof

Lies My Grandfathers Told Me

available at Inner Child Press.

www.facebook.com/gailwestonshazor
www.innerchildpress.com/gail-weston-shazor
navypoet1@gmail.com

Heaven touched earth

"And you really are
Going to make me wait"

Every minute, every day
I have become a new person
In or out of your heart
It is a magical thing, this waking up
God weaves eternity into minutes
Each new day
He makes new magic
I find that gift in your voice
In your living story
And in mine
I try to pack more meaning
Into my love
Here at the middle of all things
When my beginning is so long ago
My future is unknown
Here I want to be close to you
And find that I cannot
Because you would not have
My breath against your cheek
Though I would hold breathless
To be close to you one more time
I remember the magic of October
Recognizing my uselessness at forgetting
The only man I have ever loved
I still my hands from words
Close my eyes against the fireworks
And give in to God's stillness
My soul moves closer to yours

And it's messy and needy and honest
God answers my aches slowly
Knowing I can't handle the affirmation
In my compulsory retreat of smallness
Nursing the kind of faith
That can change lives and it's not wrong
Even though I would have you now
My heart cannot take another break
So I live in a breathless world
In and among my memories of your love
Praying that the same God
Who was faithful in answering the one prayer
Will consent to answer another one
I have never stopped loving you
Soon I will be ready
But even God knows I'm
Not yet

Primary Color

I can't really see the world this morning
As I choose to allow the light
To filter through closed lids
From grey to reds and blues
I think of the color wheels
That I have been studying
The hues mystify me in their subtleties
And today I feel like that
This not quite color
Where darkness has created a shading
Of my primary happiness
The deeper tones are always
On the inside of the wheel
Very much like where mine lie
You would miss this at a glance
Blinded by my smile
That shimmers on the edges
Of wet irises blue
And I tamp this down
Push these tones inside
To make it harder to see
The older stuff of memories
That won't fade
Though still the same happy
The same sad, the same blue
That navy started out as
Monochromatic
Complimentary
Tertiary
Complementary

Sometimes we have to believe
That we have a chameleonic choice
But the truth is
It is we
It is me
It is the I
I choose for you to see

Wet...Palindrome

Damp flight
Coursing downwards
Told Cherokee trail
Ford valleys
Crossed mountains
Bosomed babies
Child in hand
Longingly looking back
After lonesome pines
Cresting mountaintops
None home
Wet
Mother's tears
Wet
Home none
Mountaintops cresting
Pines lonesome after
Back looking lonely
Hand in child
Babies bosomed
Mountains crossed
Valleys ford
Trail Cherokee told
Downward coursing
Flight damp

Bismay
Mohanty

It took as long as decade for him to come to the forefront in the poetic world. An engineering student, a poet, a blogger, that's all Bismay Mohanty is about. Even though currently graduating in Computer Science and Engineering he aims to be the most beloved poet of the world. His works magically connect natural sceneries with romance, society, human tendencies and give rise to a sea of literary beauty. He loves to narrate his expressions and learning, therefore actively participates in literature sessions. All his dreams came true when he was nominated as a feature in YOTP by Inner Child Press.

He dreams to establish media to encourage writers and poets worldwide. Also, he aims his poems reach people all over the globe.

He can be mailed at bismaymohanty.97@gmail.com

To all men

Tonight I seek silence
For all the false promises
And unemotional attachment
Of friendship being true and permanent.
My heart is sinned and my soul is scarred
The mystery of life makes the mind from normalcy barred
Oblivion asks me to think
'Are all men happy' and winks?
Maybe not, to my dismay
Man has a hollow pushed unattended away
Breaks, he makes, and it breaks again
His being is something which his world may disdain.
I depart for the night
With my verses tight
I pray all men meet their souls, it helps
To start an early day again not for themselves.

Forever

In this score I shall set
The tale of how we met
Call it my luck or a plot of fate
Rescuing me from loneliness that I hate.

It was a new session of the year, myself I told
Fearing the chances that it may go like old
At that instance I saw a face so bright
Evading all darkness in my cold gazed sight.

The weather was coloured and my lips were pale
Yet my mind knew it has found tell-tale
And little did I knew before I was told
 catching on to my breath whilst my heart was sold.

 Never did I bid "hi" or said "goodbye"
You spoke to me with warmth of your smile
As these conversations continued long
I believed we could tag along.

Your childish mischief, innocent talk
Oh! God just wish me luck
That running mouth knew no limit
And I was the listener without much wit.

I wished we could have continued
But I can't wait more
Said those three words
With my throat still sore.

You stood still and gave a nod
Persuading me as if I made mistake
Later you blushed and said me yes
Finally, my heart had found a place.

Little did the tale continued
When the colourful moods grew grey
Though there was no feud
But you made me stand at bay.

No calls, No chats, No promises
Made me utterly plea
Soon it adds to my distress
 While u mentioned me your glee.

 I knew that we are parting
 Still prayed lord for one more blessing
You were my gift that I can't stop reminiscing
Stitching my heart as it continued breaking.

Years have passed but I still remember
Don't know if I will meet you again ever
I kept waiting and she walked away
And this is how our lives changed
forever.

To Someone

I'm too shy to bid a "hi"
When your r up close, just tell me why
It's hard to say goodbye when time flew us by
Heart sheds tears but eyes stay dry.

I help you in every way I can
Even I'm ready to endure any pain
but all pain goes in vain
when I see your smiling face, which makes me your fan.

I never deny all task u testify
No matter how difficult, I always give a try
You deny me ask with your smiling reply
This stupid mind of mine say "next time she will try".

You say you are selfish
and can never be like me
But are unable to understand that
you make me complete.

As the time goes by
It makes me clear
That I am not the one
Whom u shall make your Dear.
But I keep the promise
On this day that I will remember
Even after we part ways
We will stay friends forever.

Jackie
Davis
Allen

Jackie Davis Allen, otherwise known as Jacqueline D. Allen or Jackie Allen, grew up in the Cumberland Mountains of Appalachia. As the next eldest daughter of a coal miner father and a stay at home mother, she was the first in her family to attend college. Her siblings, in their own right, are accomplished, though she is the only one, to date, that has discovered the gift of writing.

Graduating from Radford University, with a Bachelors of Science degree in Early Education, she taught in both public and private schools. For over a decade she taught private art classes to children both in her home and at a local Art and Framing Shop where she also sold her original soft sculptured Victorian dolls and original christening gowns.

She resides in northern Virginia with her husband, taking much needed get-aways to their mountain home near the Blue Ridge Mountains, a place that evokes memories of days spent growing up in the Appalachian Mountains.

A lover of hats, she has worn many. Following marriage to her college sweetheart, and as wife, mother, grandmother, teacher, tutor, artist, writer, poet and crafter, she is a lover of art and antiques, surrounding herself, always, with books, seeking to learn more.

In 2015 she authored *Looking for Rainbows, Poetry, Prose and Art*, and in 2017, *Dark Side of the Moon*. Both books of mostly narrative poetry were published by Inner Child Press and were edited by hulya n. yilmaz.

jackiedavisallen.com
innerchildpress.com

Humbled

Restless, sleepless, beneath a blanket
Of fatigue, he tossed and turned all night

With the dawn, he found the fiend
Of insomnia's personae
Had stolen his energy

If he were being true to himself
He'd surely confess that fear of failure
Had rattled the repose of his bones
And that he simply wanted to be
Completely left alone

And, yet, as a result
Of an isolated incident, he idly perused

A pamphlet that came in the mail
In the bold print he saw enough
To stir him into action
How that came about he had no idea
He does wonder if by a simple seed

Sown long ago, belief reappeared
As from a great flood's past fears and tears

Or, whether from need or greed
Or impact from revelation. So, now
Ready to receive, and with eyes newly opened
He kneels before his bed, and confessing
Relinquishes the past and gives thanks

Alone in my Closet

The sacred echo
Reverberates in my mind

Silently it convicts me
Of the duty and blessing

Of loving actively
Of acknowledging the source

By which the gentle, persistent
Nudging of my heart

Instructs my conscious,
If you will, by faith alone

To heed the admonition
To love, to share, to do

As best as I can
That which is right

If I Were a Tree

If I were any kind of a tree
Standing alone in the midst

Of autumn's realm of season

I wonder what others might think
Seeing me mostly naked, me

Having shed my summer's attire

Perhaps they would contemplate
How it is that nature dares

To strip me down bare

Until the time of spring
When once again, thankfully

I shall be clothed in colors' green

Perhaps I would contemplate
How it is that winter's stare

Bids me conserve my energy

To hold, against my silent bark
Winter's frosty bite and simply wait

For my glory to return anew
Who knew that in autumn's
Attire, my beauty would appear

In splendiferous hues or else stripped

Down into the bones that royally reign, despite
The cold and hot, the day or the night

Despite that which is outside the landscape scene

Albert

Carrasco

Albert "Infinite the Poet" Carrasco

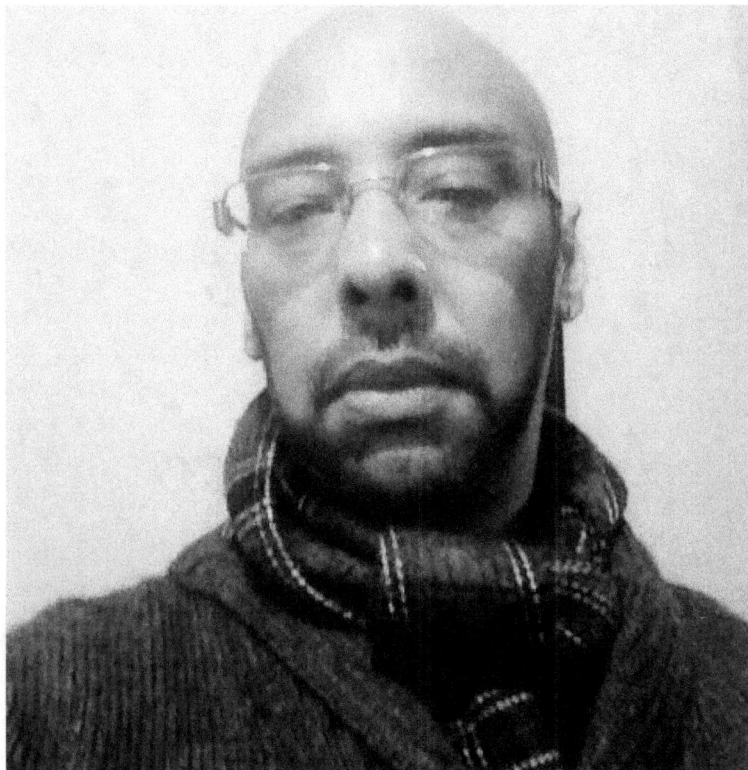

I'm a project life philanthropist, I speak about the non-ethical treatment of poor ghetto people. Why? My family was their equal, my great grandmother and great grandfather was poor, my grandmother and grandfather, my mother and father, poverty to my family was a sequel, a traditional Inheritance of the subliminal. I paid attention to the decades of regression, i tried to make change, but when I came to the fork in the road and looked at the signs that read wrong < > right, I chose the left, the wrong direction, because of street life interactions a lot around me met death or incarceration. I failed myself and others. I regret my decisions, I can't reincarnate dead men, but I can give written visions in laymens. I'm back at that fork in the road, instead of it saying wrong or right, I changed it, now it says dead men < > life.

Infinite poetry @lulu.com

Alcarrasco2 on YouTube

Infinite the poet on reverbnation

Infinite Poetry

http://www.lulu.com/us/en/shop/al-infinite-carrasco/infinite-poetry/paperback/product-21040240.html

Worrisome

Right now there's many worried children.
They're worried because their household is working on a
tight budget,
there's a lot of things they want,
but may not be able to afford it.
To the young world image is everything,
he looks nice,
she looks nice,
people saying he/she are looking like last year is what they
fear.
They don't want to sit at lunch solo,
they want to be amongst the popular kids considered the
status quo.
It's sad that not wanting to go to school because of
appearance,
is something that runs through many minds,
"if I don't get new pants,
shirts,
sneakers,
caps
etc,
I'll cut class so no one sees me".
I know well and it isn't easy.

It's the first day of school

What classes do you have? Yay, we're going to be together again! We've been in the same classes since elementary, time flies, hopefully it will remain like that during these four years in junior high. There's a bunch us. During the summer we still see each other, we are neighbors.

We go to the beach, amusement parks, camping, fishing or will just meet up in the local park and have a day of sport playing. Us being close, made our parents close, we're a huge family.

You could see the excitement in all of our eyes, guys drooling over girls, girls drooling over guys, we are all in awe over the schools size. We're freshmen and It was huge. It's something new to us. It was like a Minnie city in a big city. The halls were long and wide, the stairs steep, in between bells you can hear a stampede of feet, the rooms looked like little auditoriums, the students were all dressed nice and neat in uniform sitting calm. we're young adults now, the elementary days are gone.

Back to school

Don't cry ma, I don't need new clothes for school. Don't worry I still have space in last year's loose leaf to write in. i can tape my folders back together. I still have my pencil, pens and sharpener. No mom we don't have to borrow, we will get everything we need in one of our tomorrow's. I don't need a lunch box, just pack my sandwich in my nap sack. Mom don't worry about bus fare. I'll walk, in about a week or so my bus pass will be there. Don't worry mom I got this we will be ok. Mom why are you still crying? Mom says... I wish I could do better for such a good kid.

Joe
Da Verbal
MindDancer

Joseph L Paire' aka Joe DaVerbal Minddancer . . .
is a quiet man, born in a time where civil liberties
were a walk on thin ice. He's been a victim of his
own shyness often sidelined in his own quest for
love. He became the observer, charting life's path.
Taking note of the why, people do what they do.
His writings oft times strike a cord with the
dormant strings of the reader. His pen the rosined
bow drawn across the mind. He comes full-frontal
or in the subtlest way, always expressing in a way
that stimulate the senses.

https://www.facebook.com/joe.minddancer

BASIC LOVE

When the turn of color on leaves glow
when the first frost etches art on a pane

I'm thankful for the love in me that stares
When my neck stings from a ball of snow
I hear the giggling eyes behind the cover of home
I'm thankful for understanding, I did that too

I love the smell of plans for a feast
I thank goodness for family
I thank goodness for the ability to express
when most hearts are at rest, I dream of love

Sometimes a cloud is just a cloud
When you love for loves sake
it will never be that plain

My heart is influenced by joy and pain
I'm thankful for Sun and Rain
I'm thankful my mind is arranged to act on love

from the littlest change in nature
to a catastrophic disaster
Basic love comes together

I'm thankful I can see it
I'm hopeful we can be it
Know love and you'll receive it

HOME AND COUNTRY

The first step onto foreign land, I was thankful where I
came from
the same was said from a guy I met, He was thankful where
he came from
different laws different flaws same pause
same causes and demonstrations
same social frustrations, similar political mishandlings
it's hard to leave where you were born and raised
I'm not talking state to state or even country borders
I'm talking traveling over water
new social orders

when you see a sign from home
pride grows from your dome
you get that feeling you're not alone
The banners are waving in air
people care where they're from
people share where they're from
People protest them
People profess them
it hurts when they don't measure up
We fight when the pressures up
and will defend its honor
and not pretend, that's harder
when things are not right
But when the Sun goes down
and the land on which you stand birth stars
Be thankful where you are

THREE BUTTONS

One hole to the left of my vest
One hole, stretched at best
Beer belly tells me a size up
One button keeps my eyes up

Pressed by a pretty dress
Stressed by loveliness
Push my buttons three
Push my buttons free

There are buttons that anger me

One button keeps my eyes up
Beer belly tells me a size up
One hole, stretched at best
One hole to the left of my vest

Push my buttons free
Push my buttons free
Stressed by loveliness
Pressed by a pretty dress

there are buttons that tangle me

Push, push, push, my buttons
Elevate my status cousin
the deer are rutting

Three buttons set me free

Shareef Abdur Rasheed

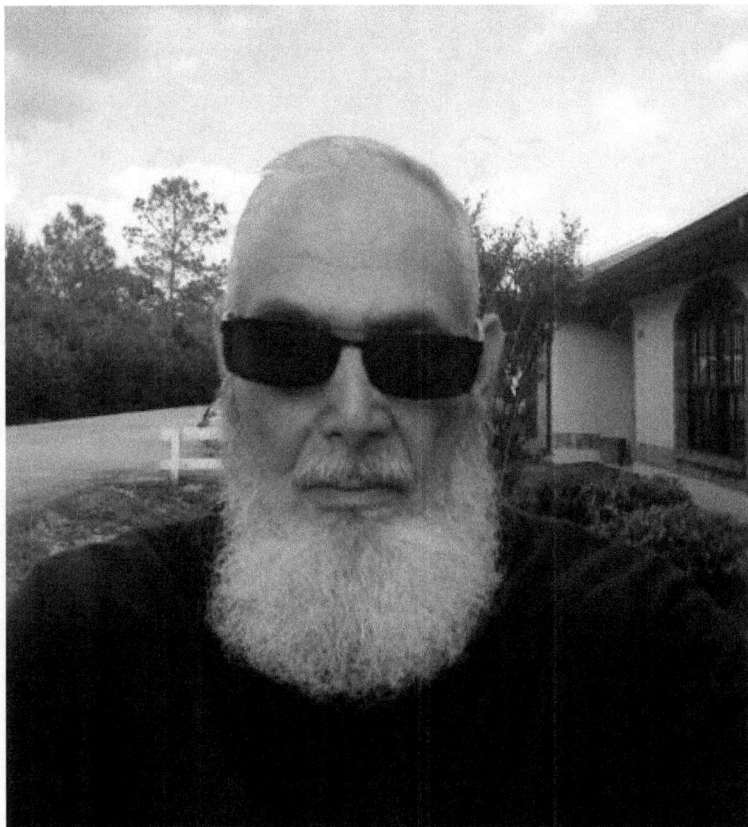

Shareef Abdur-Rasheed, AKA Zakir Flo was born and raised in Brooklyn, New York. His education includes Brooklyn College, Suffolk County Community College and Makkah, Saudi Arabia. He is a Veteran of the Viet Nam era, where in 1969 he reverted to his now reverently embraced Islamic Faith. He is very active in the Islamic community and beyond with his teachings, activism and his humanity.

Shareef's spiritual expression comes through the persona of "Zakir Flo" . Zakir is Arabic for "To remind". Never silent, Shareef Abdur-Rasheed is always dropping science, love, consciousness and signs of the time in rhyme.

Shareef is the Patriarch of the Abdur-Rasheed Family with 9 Children (6 Sons and 3 Daughters) and 41 Grandchildren (24 Boys and 17 Girls).

For more information about Shareef, visit his personal FaceBook Page at :

http://www.facebook.com/shareef.abdurrasheed
https://zakirflo.wordpress.com

inflaming..,

nation saving face in relation to all human race
consider the disgrace that awaits
implication: world's leader nation diminished reputation
because their leader was neither a decent
human being or qualified to lead
and yes you can believe..,
he, she may in fact act in collusion with evil intrusion
choosing losing over winning respect, rather disconnect
then form unity, solidarity, preserving long lasting relations
with a diversity of nations in the spirit of enhancing
humankind leaving no people behind, turning away from
doing deaf, dumb, blind way
instead using blessings bestowed to lead the way
into a brand new day
but wait a minute it was a dream had solutions to solve
problems in it
first establish justice, human rights given by the author
of rights making unity of mankind internationally the plight
but i woke up only to throw up at the sight of inept leader
acting more like bottom feeder low life
cutting freedom, peace, security, prosperity, serenity with
~~hot knife~~ causing death, sorrow, strife rather then
the above mentioned love
reason for everything, folks get leaders they deserve
based on life they chose, be it rejection or accepting
divine direction will determine mankind's fate that
ultimately
awaits affected by what path we take crooked or straight
has a direct effect on rulers being kind or who lead by hate
come correct don't sleep on cause ' n ' effect

food4thought = education

peace

please, please, please said the godfather of soul
yes please, please, please feed the soul peace
that's what souls love to eat, i repeat " that's what
souls love to eat "
speaking of love ya need a loving soul to love peace
loving soul makes one whole, it's all love beloved
never hate, except to hate hate,
evil like greed, arogance, jealousy, mischief makers
who hate peace, love war, turmoil, confusion
stop confusion, fuse the union, come together as humans
life is precious, life is short, fragile must cherish, value
every life but first cherish, value your own life, love
yourself
and you will know how to love others, value, cherish their
lives
no matter their color, tribe, nation we're all blood relation
from first human creation our father and mother of all
human race
Adam *(aws) wa Howa(ra)* our mother, our father
what da Beatles say? " Come together right now, come
together "
dismiss hate beloved, reject the request of the hater to
divide,
live off a diet of arogance, puffed up pride is no way to live
or die
instead try humility, gratitude, a loving, giving attitude
come down now off your lofty altitude, lower your wing
be a giving, caring, creator fearing, loving human being
please, please, please give peace a chance
come together right now, come together right now
bust a love nut all over the world,
bury hate before it's too late
please, please, please!

Supplicate only..,

reserved same as he who one serves exclusively,
unconditionally, repeatedly
he who one needs is he who has no needs
created all living things including their time
time to live, time to die only he knows why
supplicate only..,
to he who when he wants to do something says
" Be "
who's words are more than all waters in
all oceans, seas
hears all as well as sees all things, absolutely nothing
escapes his awareness
closer than jugular is his nearness
who, what else can be your dearest?
who else can be the fairest,
able to remove all ills at will answer: nil!
supplicate only..,
to him who is worthy of all praise, worship, devotion
including
supplication
he who hears all cries for help, the beggar who seeks
magfirah(forgiveness) he alone can forgive
is he who wants his slave who he created, fashioned, made
only to worship thee creator who is capable and actually
has created all living things that ever was ,does and will
have life unquestionable, unconditionally, totally commit
that
life which is a loan to the very one who loaned it
constantly asking help, forgiveness, guidance, protection,
sustenance, bounties, blessings

this is why he made you from nothing in the first place
but oooh sooo lost this human race, oh mankind!
looking for love in all the wrong places instead of from
he alone who made us, loaned us life will take it
for surely from Allah(swt)* we come and to him is our
return
Ameen!

food4thought = education

Kimberly
Burnham

Find yourself in the pattern. As a 28-year-old photographer, Kimberly Burnham appreciated beauty. Then an ophthalmologist diagnosed her with a genetic eye condition saying, "Consider life, if you become blind." She discovered a healing path with insight, magnificence, and vision. Today, a poet and neurosciences expert with a PhD in Integrative Medicine, Kimberly's life mission is to change the global face of brain health. Using health coaching, Reiki, Matrix Energetics, craniosacral therapy, acupressure, and energy medicine, she supports people in their healing from brain, nervous system, and chronic pain issues. As managing editor of *Inner Child Magazine*, Kimberly's 2018 project is peace poetry—*A Glossary of Peace: Perhaps If We Understood Each Other*. Featuring diverse poets, this anthology explores the nuances of peace in many languages and aims to contribute to healing in the world.

http://www.NerveWhisperer.Solutions
https://www.linkedin.com/in/kimberlyburnham

\Sensational Gratitude

Appreciate
palms together upraised
hands cooking writing
waving hugging
wrapping the world in love
experiencing delight
in peaceful touch
sought in dreams
found in every day

Gratitude for sounds
read aloud
I love you
you won
the breeze waving trees
footsteps
movement
life returning again and again
giving voice to dreams
spoken into reality

Thankfulness
see a genuine smile
lips moist
kissed by sunlight
a story poem
green branches winding
through the natural world
a tree
reaches for dreams
perceived at night
realized in morning light

Taste Treasures

Subtle spices
travelling far
cultures blending seamlessly
chocolate
hot sweet potato fries
grapes off the vine
ripe raspberries
rosemary
homegrown walnuts
crisp apples
dinner cooking
rich aromatic
fresh air near a waterfall
as water turns splashing
rising into clouds
falling again to nourish
all

Gratitude for Intuition

Right
this path
for me
a particular color
chosen from rainbows
connections made
sensations of safety
wrapped in warmth
a peace blanketing
like a layer of snow

Why
I don't know
a feeling
deep inside
subconscious made manifest
a word
a touch
a sense
this is good

Elizabeth E. Castillo

Elizabeth Esguerra Castillo is a widely-published and multi-awarded international author/poet from the Philippines. She has 2 published books: "Seasons of Emotions", UK and "Inner Reflections of the Muse", USA. Elizabeth also co-authored more than 70 international anthologies in the USA, Canada, UK, India, Romania, and Africa. Elizabeth is a member of PEN International, the American Authors Association (AAA), and Asia-Pacific Writers and Translators (APWT).

Facebook Author Page:

https://web.facebook.com/ElizabethEsguerraCastillo/

Thankfulness

Being in gratitude doesn't cost you a thing
It is deemed as a way to let blessings flood your way
To thank the Universe in every little thing you receive
The gift of life, the air you breathe,
The sun's ray kissing your cheeks, the infectious laugh of a
baby
I thank God for what I have become now
For my loving family, friends and even foes,
I thank God for my troubles which are actually blessings in
disguise
For each and every experience I take
In my journey here on earth to fulfill my Destiny.

My Vision of Love

In a secret hideaway there is where love resides
Inside the deep recesses of your whole being
Embedded in the core of your soul,
Like a caged, fragile robin
One needs to set if free and let it reign
Reign in the hearts of greedy and envious men,
Let Love rule the Land and set aside indifferences
And wake up to a brand new morn of blissful possibilities.
Let the blind see the Light and let it dawn upon him
That hatred only leads to a miserable reality,
Where there is Love, there lies Peace
My vision of Love is a world in unity
Where there is no more division, no more colors that
separate one from the other,
For we are One, from One Source
Cast out from Paradise because of one evil venom
Let Love rule our hearts and make amends with one
another
As we continue to fight the Battle together with the Angels
above
The perfect vision of love is a world in harmony
Let go of hate and set each other free.

Yearning Soul

my soul yearns for the nearness of you
to hear your voice like a beautiful melody echoing behind
the darkness,
to have your hand fit into mine
to be lost in oblivion with only you,
to look at the stars and marvel at the moon
while talking about the Universe and how you moved my
heart
my flame yearns to unite with your fire,
to ignite again the warmth of this dying ember
to get lost in your eyes, to melt with just a glimpse of your
smile
the pilgrim in me yearns to have you walk with me in my
journey,
to put an end to a dark spell with my thousand years of
waiting for only you
my soul yearns for the nearness of you.

Anna

Jakubczak

Vel Ratty

Adalan

Anna Jakubczak vel RattyAdalan – was born 18 April 1994 in Szczecin. Polish poet, journalist and the main editor of e-Magazine *Horizon*. Student on journalism and social communication at the University in Szczecin. In free time author on the website

www.annajakubczak.wordpress.com

Anna Jakubczak vel RattyAdalan collaborate with Association of Polish Writers and few Polish and international magazines. Her poems were included in a few American anthologies: „FM 7: Fall 2013", „FM 8: Winter", „FM 9: Spring 2014", „FM 12: Summer 2015" and "FM 13: Fall 2016" published by Lewis Crystal and Roseanne Terranova Cirigliano in cooperation with Publishing House „Avenue U Publications" and She started to publish her poetry in the cycle "The Year of The Poet" since 2016. Poem "Interlova" was printed in the magazine "The Indus Streams" published by Apeejay Stya University (School of Journalism & Mass Communication).

She's interested in philosophy, literature, psychology, music, mass media. Her hobbies are: cooking, reading books, learning foreign languages, translating and traveling.

In 2013 she published her debut volume: „Ars Poetica". At now she's working on next books: volume "Conversation at night", novel "Wind of hope", collection of stories "Gates of subconscious" and fairytales "The squirrel's stories from the old larch".

Novenna
.... For Mother

I'm like a cat in empty apartament,
don't believe that the door
will not open any more.
You left so quietly, unexpectedly,
didn't tell why so early.

Is the fate has invited you to tea,
so you with Poswiatowska
could enjoy the fine metaphors.
Or maybe has the God
appointed you another job?

Oh God although I'm sad, I'll miss you
curled up like a cat, by the empty bowl.
Playing with reflection, listen
for the steps that will never come.

God, take care of her
and you will take care of me as well.

Sanctuary

bitterness
lurks insidiously to the dream
and the time
in which disappears
image of the last dance
singing is lasting:
let perpetual light shine…

certificate
between flames
and cross – positive
at which bounces off the wind

there are also spiders
winter caretakers, weaving duvets
to not have experience the frost
eternally alive names of the nature

ab ovo usque ad mala*

Latin – from start to finish

I'll wait
...For Arsenie

Although there will be a day
when I already wither.
When the night will not be dependent
on the day.
And the soul I will hang up
as he frayed coat.
I'll wait.

Although you already forget.
Another as smooth as silk
will touch your face
and all poems turn into yellowish.
I' ll wait.

And the inspiration
the wind can take somewhere,
throwing dust on the tombstone,
which will emboss the epitaph,
telling all in just one word.
I'll wait.

Nizar

Sartawi

Nizar Sartawi is a poet, translator and educator. He was born in Sarta, Palestine, in 1951. He holds a Bachelor's degree in English Literature from the University of Jordan, Amman, and a Master's degree in Human Resources Development from the University of Minnesota, the U.S. Sartawi is a member of the Jordanian Writers Association, General Union of Arab Writers, and Asian-African Writers Union. He has participated in poetry readings and international forums and festivals in Jordan, Lebanon, Kosovo, and Palestine, and Morocco.

Sartawi's first poetry collection, **Between Two Eras**, was published in Beirut, Lebanon in 2011. His poetry translations into Arabic include: **The Prayers of the Nightingale** (2013), poems by Indian poet Sarojini Naidu; **Fragments of the Moon** (2013), poems by Italian poet Mario Rigli; **The Souls Dances in its Cradle** (2015), poems by Danish poet Niels Hav; **Searching for Bridges** (2013), poems by American poet Margaret Saine (2016) **The Talhamiya** (2016), poems by Palestinian poet Nathalie Handal. His Arabic poetry translations into English include **Contemporary Jordanian Poets**, Volume I (2013); **The Eyes of the Wind** (2014), poems by Tunisian poet Fadhila Masaai; **The Birth of a Poet** (2015, 2016), poems by Lebanese poet Mohammad Ikbal Harb; **Haifa and other Poems** (2016), poems by Palestinian poet Samih Masaud; **The Pearls of a Grief** (2016), poems by Lebanese poet Abdulkarim Baalbaki. He has also been working for the last four years on a translation project, Arab Contemporary Poets Series.

Sartawi's poems and translations have been anthologized and published in books, journals, and newspapers in Arab countries, the U.S., Australia, Indonesia, Italy, the Philippines, and India.

Broken Olive

a bleeding branch
of a maimed
olive tree
lying beside
the road

a stranger
passing by
asks: WHY?

a crowd
of angry faces
shaking
in dismay

four men in a jeep
watching silently
fingers on the triggers

and from above
a lonely dove
spits
an olive leaf

* * * *

Genesis

And now
that spirit has been breathèd
into her nares
all of a sudden
she breaks
out of her shell
and there emerges she
an awkward princess
awakened from her sleep.

She stretches
her wings –
small and soft –
and makes as if to fly.

~ ~ ~ ~

O little child
your downy coat
has not as yet feathered.

Nor has my pencil
hitherto
declared you
daughter of my dreams

* * * *

Motherless Day

On your Day,
Mother
I drag my legs
to the narrow spot
where my eyes looked once
upon your holy corpse
swaddled in white
and laid deep
 in your great Mother's bosom.

How much did I ever give back?:
a handful of dust
dispersed
upon the white sheet

Two salty drops
moisten my lips
as I walk away
drooping my head
a helpless
homeless
dog!

      * * * *

Ten Walls

Jen Walls

Jen Walls is a celebrated international author, poet, editor, and literary reviewer/critic. Jen brings heart-radiance alive; pulsating mystical poetry as soul's sharing care of rare positivity. Jen's first collection, *The Tender Petals*, was released November 2014 by inner child press, Ltd. USA. Her second book of poems, *OM Santih Santih Santih*, featured co-authored spiritual nature duet poems that sing of love and peace from both author's solo and combined poetic works. *OM Santih* was released in November 2015 by The Poetry Society of India. She brings heart blessings onto grace-journeys via mystical nature poetry; shimmering beauty that glides forth - meeting love-vibes held compassionately through positive poetic mantra-verses. She joyfully writes daily on Facebook; utilizing it as a vibrant and living poetic palette. Jen's works appear globally in renowned anthologies and international literary publications. A few include: *Contemporary Vibes, PoetCrit, Bhakti Blossoms, Core Realm of Cosmic Peace & Harmony, The Year of the Poet,* and *The Martin Lake Journal*. Her poems are dedicated conscious breaths to awaken living prayers for our world peace and global harmony. Jen was awarded the 2016 Distinguished Poet Award from Writers International Network (WIN-Canada). She devotionally flows profound love-messages for the entire humanity. Jen resides in Saint Paul, Minnesota, USA with her loving family.

Contact Jen Walls: mywritegift@gmail.com

https://www.facebook.com/jen.walls.7
http://www.innerchildpress.com/jen-walls.php

HEART OF DIVINE

Supreme Love's found in the selfless Self
lives on - praying inside bubbling fresh dew
ever awakening - through and through
into light, the day brings each living gift.
We're here learning how we're to be true
within opening waves, finding love's heart
unwrapping petals - perfuming perfect kiss
watching, we wake the eye of consciousness.
Eclipse and learn to outgrow our ignorance
reach within - touch-find sun's cosmic rays
weave a dance - feel beyond dreaming-spray
live free, bringing light into each truthful day.
Abide with soul's mantle and raise love high
birth's not to be in vain, nor is death just to fly
Mother gives her touch to calm all the cries
soothing lifetimes from storming rage and fear.
Heartbeats sing, share a caress lingering here
breathing an ancient song, loving and strong
only love-birds call out to find one another
resounding prayers, living in earthen mists.
Eternity persists - greeting the love-breaths
meeting melts of heart through infinite grace
speak silent flows - loving soundless sound
give sublime bliss-surround into heart of divine.

HEART'S HAPPENING

Perceive divine dew
pray creative spirit through;
shine living-joy breaths

Pace with sunny calm
melt light-sprays across heart's lake;
receive sweet-flow streams

Breathe-be loving peace
hear through soul - beauty's prayer;
know love's silent care

Quiet - live restful
whisper peace with everything;
feel care-balm's calm grace

Blaze fire - go through
burst beauty beyond thinking;
lift in glowing hope

Wake full coloring
watch turn of autumn arrive;
dance heart's happening

INNER-SUN

Be watchful - blaze light
clear windows of translucence
feel breaths that are known

Bloom gratitude's bliss
flow heart's nectar - share beauty;
wake spiritual peace

Melt-away morn's frost
dance simply seraphic flight;
drip effortless dew

Watch sweet bloom come true
give heart's cup overflowing;
live bliss - O' Sadhu

Fly love into heights
carry kiss alive - thrive joy;
wake the inner-sun

hülya

n.

yılmaz

A Penn State faculty in Humanities, published author, literary translator and freelance editor, hülya n. yılmaz started her formal writing career in the U.S. after joining the Nittany Valley Writers Network in Centre County, PA. Her poetry made its first public appearance in the OLLI Magazine, *Pastiche*. Dr. yılmaz' academic publications include an extensive research book on the literary relations between the West and the Islamic East, a chapter for a book of critical essays on Orhan Pamuk – the recipient of the 2006 Nobel Prize in Literature, and several treatises presented at national and international conferences.

Outside the academia, hülya has authored *Trance*, a book of poetry in Turkish, German and English, and co-authored another collection of poems, *An Aegean Breeze of Peace* with Demetrius Trifiatis, professor of Philosophy from Greece. She finds it vital for everyone to understand a deeper self and writes creatively to attain and nourish it.

Links

Personal Web Site
http://authoroftrance.com

Personal Blog Site
https://dolunaylaben.wordpress.com

giving thanks? an understatement!

1

in an intense relationship
since last May
with nature oh so divine
all that i had missed for too many years
catching up now with its wonders
any second that i can
and i can do so quite well
i came to realize

thankful
grateful
utterly appreciative
that she held my hand to lead the way
to live and love the now and the here

do i no longer dwell in the past
oh yes i do
it is a different commemoration though
my beloveds gone to soon
. . . or timely as some might conclude . . .
would have wanted nothing but
peace from within for me
they will know after all
i am celebrating
their lives my to-be-ensuing death
all that which they gifted me with
no longer trapped in those

self-destructive sorrows of mine
but rather fiercely making up
for lost time
basking in their
incomparably precious memories
thanking them
at the core of my soul
our spirits thus unite in awe
for each other's good

oh yes i will be okay
everything shall be alright
because there indeed is a might
that oversees them me us
in a constant delight

so my self i find
inside a reunion of eternal light
and i thank life
i thank
i thank
i thank

2

had i known
would i have grown
this clueless all these years

3
thankful gratitude
for i can appreciate
life and death while whole

Teresa

E.

Gallion

Teresa E. Gallion was born in Shreveport, Louisiana and moved to Illinois at the age of 15. She completed her undergraduate training at the University of Illinois Chicago and received her master's degree in Psychology from Bowling Green State University in Ohio. She retired from New Mexico state government in 2012.

She moved to New Mexico in 1987. While writing sporadically for many years, in 1998 she started reading her work in the local Albuquerque poetry community. She has been a featured reader at local coffee houses, bookstores, art galleries, museums, libraries, Outpost Performance Space, the Route 66 Festival in 2001 and the State of Oklahoma's Poetry Festival in Cheyenne, Oklahoma in 2004. She occasionally hosts an open mic.

Teresa's work is published in numerous Journals and anthologies. She has two CDs: *On the Wings of the Wind* and *Poems from Chasing Light*. She has published three books: *Walking Sacred Ground, Contemplation in the High Desert* and *Chasing Light.*

Chasing Light was a finalist in the 2013 New Mexico/Arizona Book Awards.

The surreal high desert landscape and her personal spiritual journey influence the writing of this Albuquerque poet. When she is not writing, she is committed to hiking the enchanted landscapes of New Mexico. You may preview her work at

http://bit.ly/1aIVPNq or *http://bit.ly/13IMLGh*

High Desert Moment

The clouds rush toward the plains
with a song in their wings.
I want to hitch a ride as they chase
green streaking across the valley.

A tease of yellow chamisa flirts
between the desert grass.
As summer winds down,
fall takes its yearly stroll.

Gratitude bursts from my chest
in uncontrolled waves
as the fall festival begins.
I am here to witness the change.

Little Bird

She calls my name
with such a sweet chirp.

I walk closer to her and
she does not fly away.

She feels the flood of love's energy
around me and draws near.

I am humbled by her gift of song
embracing the breeze.

I am blessed to encounter her
and gratitude flows from my eyelids.

When you see a little bird,
always give it a big smile.

The Punishment Room

The image of the punishment corner
lives with me even today.
My mother did not believe in spankings.

Depriving me of the outdoors worked much
better until I adjusted to sitting quietly
on a yellow soft stool facing the wall.

When Mama forgot to check on me,
there was always writing on the wall.
Though I disliked not going outside to play,

staring at a white wall became a great place.
I travel to exotic places like Africa and dance
with the natives, paddle down the Amazon River

with an indigenous tribe or beat the hell out
of someone as a ninja warrior. My imagination
came alive sitting in the corner.

I was an avid reader of National Geographic
and anything else that involved travel.
Momma did not realize that at some point

the punishment no longer worked until
the day she tried to get my attention.
She yelled my name and I did not respond.

She understood why I was so quiet.
I had zoned out to travel. She physically shook
me back to that corner in the living room.

A new punishment method later evolved.

Faleeha

Hassan

Faleeha Hassan is a poet, teacher, editor, writer born in Najaf, Iraq, in 1967, who now lives in the United States.

Faleeha's poetry has been translated into English, Turkmen, Bosevih, Indian, French, Italian, German, Kurdish, Spain and Albanian. She has received many Arabic awards throughout he writing career.

Her poems and her stories published in different American magazines Such as : Philadelphia poets 22, Harbinger Asylum , Brooklyn Rail April 2016, Screaminmamas, The Galway Review, Words without Borders, TXTOBJX, intranslation, SJ .magazine, nondoc ,Wordgathering , SCARLET LEAF REVIEW , Courier-Post , I am not a silent poet, taosjournal, Inner Child Press , Press of Atlantic City.

d.fh88@yahoo.com

The Futility of Protesting Near Bustling Cemeteries

For the Most Important Person in My Life, My Son Ahmad

Preamble:

Take my spirit for your shirt
And use my heart's arteries for shoelaces.

Poem

My spirit patched with raw dreams,
My soft body blemished by war's scars,
My heart crushed and crunched like
Leaves under foot—
These are the sole signs of my existence
In a room that awaits a hurricane
That dreams of unleashing its gales.

My son,
Let me say tonight,
Objectively,
That I can't do anything more.
What happens,
Happens all the time.
What doesn't happen,
Never happens,
But we always paint a comely face
On life's hideous visage.

Remembering

I remember

I was born there,

Near a lingering dream,

When my mother, alone with her passion,

(I 'm alone still, an orphan)

Arranged her dreams in boxes called "us"

And then returned the next morning to

Press her eyes to shed kohl,

While she slept, we lay as naked as a freshly washed tunic

Inhaling alienation as we dried.

The Wagon

So Like a man inured to failure,
We climbed aboard the wagon,
And The driver, only the driver,
Began to listen as the cadence of our deprivation
—Thud. . .. Clunk. . . and so on-
-Infiltrated the wagon's pores,
Starting with that first dirt road.
Our lives' parasols disappointed us
When we shared sorrows
Without fancy titles,
while Reaping lethargy and frustration.
It wasn't only the driver, or The horse, or Our heads
That looked meager;
The wagon's outlook did too.

Translated by William M. Hutchins

Caroline

Nazareno

Caroline Nazareno-Gabis a.k.a. Ceri Naz, born in Anda, Pangasinan, Philippines, known as a 'poet of peace and friendship', is a multi-awarded poet, editor, publicist, linguist, and educator.

Graduated cum laude with the degree of Bachelor of Elementary Education, specialized in General Science at Pangasinan State University. Ceri has been a voracious researcher in various arts, science and literature. Recognized as dedicated volunteer of Richmond Multicultural Concerns Society, TELUS World Science, Vancouver Art Gallery, Vancouver Aquarium and some charity foundations in Canada and in the Philippines.

Beyond her Directorships in Writers Capital International Foundation (WCIF), World Poetry Canada International and Galaktika ATUNIS, she advocates peace, women's rights, culture, arts and literature: Global Citizen's Initiatives, Asia Pacific Writers and Translators *(APWT)*; The Poetry Posse, Association for Women's Rights in Development *(AWID)*, Universal Peace Federation, Akademika Nusa International Social Sciences and Humanities *(ANISSH)*, Axlepino and Anacbanua.

Her poems were published in various local prints and international anthologies. Among the prestigious awards she received are: 4th Place in World Union of Poets Poetry Prize with 100 participants worldwide, Writers International Network-Canada ''Amazing Poet 2015'', The Frang Bardhi Literary Prize 2014 (Albania), the sair-gazeteci or Poet-Journalist Award 2014 (Tuzla, Istanbul, Turkey) and World Poetry Empowered Poet 2013 (Vancouver, Canada).

Uno, on Your Birthday

Let me write you a welcome note
Just for you, today—
you are a miracle and wonder
with your first cry, first stretch,
first warm reddish dimple show
and angel's smile,
You are God's perfect breath of love
as your parents' number one and first born
The beginning of joy
The heaven's heart, baby Uno!

portrait of gratitude: first family picture

those faces smiling

are like rhythmic flames in a canvas

the best sketch framed in gratitude—

the father, the mother and the son

with the best colours running through

the symphonic first family picture,

the best moment being treasured,

the best photo of the day

that reflects the goodness

of the Great Almighty.

Euphoria 10.17.2017

For today, you can see his tiny fingers

So gently closed,

His baby scented, milky blue-white striped socks

Invite tender loving care…

The second day we meet,

You are asleep, as we welcome you home,

You're in the arms of your loving Grandma

as I lift the big umbrella,

Those chinky little eyes

are like reviving innocent crepuscular rays,

and when I see your face,

 it carries brimming galaxies.

William

S.

Peters Sr.

Bill's writing career spans a period of over 50 years. Being first Published in 1972, Bill has since went on to Author in excess of 40 additional Volumes of Poetry, Short Stories, etc., expressing his thoughts on matters of the Heart, Spirit, Consciousness and Humanity. His primary focus is that of Love, Peace and Understanding!

Bill says . . .

I have always likened Life to that of a Garden. So, for me, Life is simply about the Seeds we Sow and Nourish. All things we "Think and Do", will "Be" Cause and eventually manifest itself to being an "Effect" within our own personal "Existences" and "Experiences" . . . whether it be Fruit, Flowers, Weeds or Barren Landscapes! Bill highly regards the Fruits of his Labor and wishes that everyone would thus go on to plant "Lovely" Seeds on "Good Ground" in their own Gardens of Life!

to connect with Bill, he is all things Inner Child

www.iaminnerchild.com

Personal Web Site

www.iamjustbill.com

Remembering Thanksgiving

i sit here in this quiet place
remembering when
my brothers and my Sisters
were children
and the hustle and bustle
that went along with the times

there was the Thanksgiving Day Parade
with Lit's Brothers and John Wannamaker
ushering in the Christmas Season
and the expectations
that went along

we did not know of commerce then
nor do i think we would have cared
for to us, Santa Claus was real
it did not cost us nothing
but a few weeks of good behaviour
and plenty of prayers

after the festivities
of the marchers and music
and the band and clowns
and flowered floats
we made our way back home

Cranberry Sauce and Turkey

i remember the smells
in the entire neighborhood
for everyone had the same agenda
we could follow the fragrance
of basted Turkey and Stuffing
from the time we got off of
the 11 Trolley,

down the street
and straight to the Dining Room

"Wash your hands !"
i still hear those words
of instruction
with a slight tinge of demand
coming from Pauline's mouth.
Mom

Apron tied around her waist
hair all over her face
as we took our place
at the table

Cranberry Sauce
that was what i wanted

As time went on
and we grew up
to go our separate ways
the same scene played again
every year
only these times
the roles were reversed
we now were the parents
telling and yelling
"Wash You Hands"

We so loved the preparation
from the shopping for the fare
to the when we prepared
for this glorious day

Turkey,
Stuffing,
Greens,

Corn Pudding,
Macaroni and Cheese,
Corn Bread & Rolls
Sweet Potatoes
and let us not forget
Cranberry Sauce

Yes, those were the times

So, now here i sit
in the quiet
reflecting
on those times

Mom has since crossed over
as did Virisa,
the Mother of my 8 Children
and they now have their own agendas

My oldest 3 daughters
are now playing the roles them selves
for their Mother Janice
lives in a different State
and she gets to play Grandmom
you know,
an advisory role, Director
of the script

there is no one around,
but i am thankful for my Sister Cindy
for she included me this day
in her play
and brought me over a wonderful plate
filled with wonder
and good food

but she forgot the Cranberry Sauce
but that is OK
'cause i have a half
of a Sweet Potato Pie
she baked
and i am going to sit down
and pretend to be a Turkey
and stuff my self

yes,
i am remembering Thanksgiving
and those moments
i will not let go

the quiet takes a bit to get used to
even after all these years
but as i said
i remember thanksgiving
and i am thankful to have had . . .

i give thanks

i carefully laid my burlap sack
upon the earthen floor
of our home
preparing my self
for escape

our bellies though not full
did not complain
for the gruel abated
our misery

i humbled my spirit
of the day
into the realm of reverence
and i gave thanks
for again
i have made it through

my parents could not afford
a padded mat
for sleep
for us children
and i at times
cursed our circumstance
wrongly
for they still slept
upon Mother's nakedness

soon the new day will be calling
and we knew what that held for us

we have learned to smile
in the face of the day
and we embrace the sunshine
with joy

and we smile
for God is speaking to us too

we have come to trust in our destiny
and we held to our hope
that some day . . .
we would have a mattress
with a pillow
and blankets
to stave off the coolness of night
and perhaps we will go
to the respite of the night
with full stomachs

but in the mean time
i am grateful
for what little we do have
and i am open to receive
what may come
for anything that does come about
represents increase
and an opportunity
to give more thanks.

i give thanks

Thankfulness in the fields of the Lorde

God has stayed my hand
when i could not
helped me to remember the blessings
i forgot
slowed my pace
when i was ready to trot
to a quasi wizened man
from that innocent tot

i was hungry
and i was fed
i was lost
and i was led
a spirit of loneliness
to spirit wed
with a certain peace
i lie upon this bed

there's a beauty contained
in each moment of each day
through my despair
He makes a way
i am Blessed and Blessing
is what i say
the life i choose
i'm a child play

in the fields of the Lorde

World Healing, World Peace
2018

World Healing World Peace

2018

POEtRy

i am a believer !

www.worldhealingworldpeacepoetry.com

Submission Guidelines

1 Poem

Microsoft Word Attachment (NO PDF's)

12 pt. Times Roman

Titles Underlined

Single Spaced

Maximum 30 lines

Picture of Poet (no avatars or icons accepted)

Biography 50 words or less with maximum 2 Web Links

Submit to :

worldhealingworldpeace@gmail.com

Submissions open from September 1st ~ December 31st, 2017

Publishing for International Poetry Month April 2018

www.worldhealingworldpeacepoetry.com

Project Manager : Gail Weston Shazor

Underwritten by Inner Child Press

Now Open for submissions
until December 31st, 2017

November 2017

Features

~ * ~

Kay Peters

Alfreda D. Ghee

Gabriella Garofalo

Rosemary Cappello

Kay
Peters

Kay Peters

Kay Peters' poems have been published in Apiary, U.S. 1 Worksheets, Philadelphia Poets, Mad Poets Review, Philadelphia Stories, Schuylkill Valley Journal and the online journal Word Gathering. She is a recipient of the Petracca Family Award presented by Philadelphia Poets.

Kay is a registered nurse, a former Oncology Clinical Nurse Specialist who now practices as a parish nurse in her church. Kay is a wannabe gardener who spends more time pulling weeds than growing the flowers and herbs that she loves.

RESURRECTION

*After Prison Uprising at Qala I Jangi, Afganistan by Alex
Perry and Dodge Billingsley*

They seem to take for granted their spring miracle,
> *journalists report an uprising of Taliban prisoners,*
those turtles on the log warming the sculpted stone of their
shells.
> *an airstrike screams in— misses its target*

I want to take for granted the sun after winter,
> *gunfire and explosions fill the night,*
instead I wonder when it is time for them to descend into
darkness,
> *in morning bodies litter the compound—*

as they breathe a sigh of bubbles that rise like pearls to the
surface,
> *rocket propelled grenades fired into the prison*
are they aware that their night is not forever?
> *oil is poured in and set on fire,*

What knowledge can they have that they will rise from
their cold beds?
> *the prison is flooded with ice water — Taliban
> surrender,*
They do not know about the death,
> *"You can't just push a button to end this… you have
> to look the men in the eye that you are going to
> kill",*

the stone rolled back— the grave empty.

OUR TOWN'S MEMORIAL

A blackened girder
twisted like ribbon
stands at the center.

Touch it.
Does it shudder
with the impact?
Can you feel the heat
of jet- fueled flames?

Move closer.
Can you hear
screams and prayers
as the steel skeleton
falls to its knees
in a cloud of toxic dust?

MISINFORMATION

They said after
black-winged words
fledged from the mouths
of the powerful.

We scarcely noticed
when shadows
fell across our tables
and power lines sagged
beneath the weight of deceit.

Then we heard the harsh
caw-caw and felt
cold wind stirred
by frenzied wings,

And when we looked
mourners were gathering
like dark clouds
on the horizon.

Alfreda
D.
Ghee

Alfreda D. Ghee

My name is Alfreda Ghee. I'm an Author, poet a friend to many and most of all a mother of 2 amazing sons. I run my own home daycare in hopes to providing a safe place for kids of all ages. I live life to the fullest and appreciate all things life has to offer. I seek to provide a positive light in my life and my family and friends lives. Living life is to give love to all things, beings and creatures God have created and will create. To know life is to appreciate living and to have Lived, life is to Love what you know and what you are willing to learn and change in your life first and in others lives in a positive direction..

Kisses

Your last kiss
Was like your first kiss
It lingered in mind
Sent time sprawling into a whirl wind
Into deep space
As my thoughts raced in hast
To understand the demands of emotions formed…

Your last kiss
Was like your first kiss
On my collar bone
It sent shivers down my spine
Time went rewind and came and came to a stand still
As my mind flooded with visions of impurities
My senses were heighten
And full of life….

Your first kiss
Was like your last kiss
The earth stopped spinning
All existence was no more
The heavens opened
And the angels song a song of glorious expectations
As my mind was frozen in time
I couldn't verbalize
The tidal wave of emotions over riding
      My insides,
      My soul
      My entire being

Leaving me stunned
From the realization that time has become undone
All because of your first kiss being our last……

Fear

His soul aches for its missing link
It hears no sound
Except the beating of its own thoughts
It sees only his breath in the air
As if it was a cold winters night..

Life seems to slow down
The earth doesn't move under his feet
It pains him….. Because
The chirping isn't heard from the birds
Laughter isn't heard from the children at play
And the good things didn't last…

All the while death, darkness and rust
Has corroded his surroundings
Trying to drain his life force
Torn between two halves of right and wrong
His soul has slumpt and turned to coal…

Fighting to return to an existence
Of being whole
Not sure of the path he has chosen
Shaking in fear
With tears streaming down his face
Because he knows an intervention of his relapse
Is needed..

To open his heart to the light he imagines is in the distance
Not able to touch nor feel its warmth
His soul has gone cold
Waiting for him to reach out and claim the truth
That the darkness only came
When he set his soul on the back of the shelf
To search for a missing link he never lost……

Secrets

My tear stained pillow is heavy
It tries to disguise my thoughts
It holds the secrets of my dreams
Filled with disdain and shame..

My emotional mattress
Is over loaded with disgust and miss guided trust
That's flustered and stained
From being used and abused..

The comfort of my covers
Don't engulf my securities and make me feel safe
It houses my insecurities
The unrest and unjust
They are left within the sheets
Where my secret identity is held for keeps
As it seeps through and question my judgment
To my surprise the walls keeps it all
While the fan blows it all in the wind....

Gabriella Garofalo

Born in Italy some decades ago, Gabriella Garofalo fell in love with the English language at six, started writing poems (in Italian) at six and is the author of "Lo sguardo di Orfeo"; "L'inverno di vetro"; "Di altre stelle polari"; "Blue branches".

Blue

A blue Ukyyoe walking in a haze,
We are crossing a fleeting border where they wave 'Hello'
Out of the blue and you judder, so lost in your thoughts
On the latest fad, guys giving shape to steel, words, clay,
Whatever, they call 'em artists, right?
Now listen to this, and no, I kid you not,
As soon as the job's done they jump the border
In a trail of blaze -
Maybe fire, though life sticks to her blue and says no -
Those dreamy la-la landers!
What? Love, mercy, compassion?
No, afraid you can't grasp such exotic idiom
If a necropolis of Etruscan smiles, your soul,
Is waiting for the sentence -
Yes, tonight and don't you dare kid yourself
Stars can help, they're idling time in crumbling mansions
Where they give out light for free -
But he's standing still, Hesperus too scared
To let his love glide over the Moon -
Go, I shout him, go, you jerk,
For the light of regret lurks white in the corners,
Don't let her light up your house,
Whatever left behind goes pouf and you, winter,
You rotten season stop with your deaf twilights,
No sign language here, I can't talk,
Get rid of them, quick, chatting with Hesperus and the
Moon
Got my goat, and I'm dying, I'm dying I say
For fresh words, dancing gabs,
And I'm no match-maker, you know?

Oh, and those bells chiming at mid-morning or eventide,
How do I feel for the Angels moaning
When those meddling sounds
Make their chords a cheap medley no one listens to,
Why don't they stop it? That, and the pewter scud
Banking over the sky like an obsessive father -
But no they say, no, and the Moon too says no
To the evening star -
Of course, if she isn't already dashing
To some secret lover for a bit of whoopee.

Afternoon Madness

I know, they call for a price
Your breath the very sec you wake up,
Every dawn a bloody toddler screaming
For Mummy to give him food -
The day the vet had killed a feral cat
The doctor told me to avoid stress, bright lights,
Even life if I could, 'cept I had no one
To stop me from walking on,
The cars from speeding up,
The sparks from kindling minds -
'T was then it dawned on me
How wicked is an afternoon's madness,
But short on words to nice up dreams,
On fearful ravens to warm to my days,
I flung my soul to the sky like a falcon
Spurting fear over windswept hills,
Blind to the moon who looked
As a five-something child had doodled it -
Shame she was so helpless
Against the dark nicking death from sneers and maids -
Wait, no death of course, as my soul told me once back,
Only a frosty ground where life kept growing
And didn't I like the earth
With her golden heart and fruits aplenty?
Man was I feeling dizzy from anger and noise,
Yet I made it, I got it, but I hadn't the foggiest,
It simply grows, innocence, a sorry lack of wit, darkness?
Oh I almost forgot, you ever noticed
Young couples in love always sport
A maudlin smile when snapped together?
What do you think? Bit of a drag I'd say,
But of course I might be wrong.

Spring

What can spring do,
But scolding butterflies when they act funny -
High on wind or flowers?
Maybe, or so I heard
Some fretful goody goodys whisper
While I was waiting for the manager
To ask who gave me that bloodiest gift,
Birth:
Was it a scam or a sudden whim
To get rid of damaged goods, my soul?
And don't get me started on those letters,
Words, words, the chief mourners in a grim look,
'I'd like to help, but am bit skint', this
'Sorry I can't lend you bit o' dosh,' that -
Smiling waves and muah muah over
Off to delis or a fashion boutiques,
Dinners and parties the very soul of life,
Don't you know? No, you don't -
O sweet inconsistency, my precious charade,
Don't ask why pewter skies worry me,
I've always lived winters as fussy managers
In charge of storms, dark and frost,
Or conjurers dying to blast us
With gleeful sunny spells -
But I don't do that business, no answers for me
So I collect green bits of hope,
Green hankies and scraps of paper,
Only they hold a grudge against God,
His fields, his dandelions,
An icy stare the only help I get,
I feel lost, what else, and avert mine -
And yes, that's where I live,

Where April winds slay windmills and kites -
They tee him off while he's mooning
At the TV screen;
And yes, that's where I live,
Where August heat shuts up the music -
Don't stars need silence to pray;
And yes, that's where I live,
Where October sun gathers a bevy of pundits
Who tell us how and what to think,
See their groupies stumbling over the stilettos
After boozing it up?
Time to listen now, you, first lovers,
You, spooky jeans-clad bimbos,
You, witches incognito or vixens in disguise:
All rookies, OK, but saving the tree of life?
Sure, it's old, eternal, at risk,
But, really, newbies meddling in such dicey jobs?
Why the heck you got muddled in that screw-up?
Adam, Eve, look at your kids,
Madness and poetry hassling a plump lady
Waiting for her coffee -
Oh, it's me among season fruits, treats and threats,
Before the fall, a ruthless cobalt blue,
The wrath of wandering lights,
Maybe the look of drifting -
'Today the light is dancing around you'
Goes all chirps a socialite wannabe writer -
Sorry? Beloved, if I get it fine,
The light whenever the hand
Strikes dead the soul.

Rosemary
Cappello

Rosemary Cappello is a writer/poet Rosemary Cappello lives in Philadelphia, Pennsylvania.

Rosemary is a Poet, Writer, Watercolorist, and the Editor of "Philadelphia Poets".

She attended at Widener University and is a graduate of the Class of 1983 where she studied English/Creative Writing and Anthropology. Rosemary also wrote film reviews and interviews for "The Dome" in Chester, Pennsylvania

ODE TO A DEAD WISTERIA

Your trunk so mighty remains
like a human torso withered with age. This spring,
your trunk has not grown the arms
of floral branches, no fingers
of vivid, splendid aromatic blooms.
Just a twisted trunk with thick thighs that
curve down to crawling legs where—who knows?
a nanogram of life could be contained,
could burst forth again.

Till then, there you are,
o once glorious wisteria,
like a Greek god decapitated and deflowered,
and yet, still glorious.

The Nurturer

I often wonder how he grew to be so nurturing, the way
he took all people into his comfortable arms,
cooked Russian peasant meals for friends and family.

He'd received no tenderness from his mother,
referred to her as a "neurotic invalid" living in
another world. As for his father, he was

a rough and brutal man, starting from the early morning
hour
when he shouted his children awake, sending them to work
in the family business before school started.

My friend was different from his parents. Never got angry.
Never judged others. He'd say a mean person was "more to
be
pitied than censured."

That seems like a lyric from a 19th century song,
humorous-sounding to our later times,
but he said it from deep thought,

applied it to his parents, understood and forgave them,
grew up to be a nurturer.

FOR MY FRIEND, DYING

I think of how people who are still Catholics—and even
some who are not—
will send sacred objects to someone who is ill. Not having
them on hand
I would search the world for them for you—
a splinter of the true cross, a sliver of a great saint's bones,
St. Rita's oil, Lourdes water; fragments and vials of blessed
objects
meant to heal the sick. But I can just hear you dismissing
this idea.

I wonder about those who discarded their crutches at
Lourdes—
did they walk, run, jump, hop for the rest of their lives after
being crippled,
or was it just that one moment of ecstasy, lifting them
above their mortal state,
making them feel whole: that shout of joy, that feeling of
wellbeing lasting
but a moment. Were they photographed in that one brief
second and the
word spread that they were cured, or were they really
healed for all time?

When not feeling well, I sleep with my rosary beads, the
ones
my sister Jo made for me, with a special crucifix and
Blessed Mother medal
she chose specifically for me. Pink beads. They console
me, and I remember
when my sister Jo couldn't speak anymore, she began
tracing words in the air.

My son Joe gave her paper and pencil and she wrote "I love
you so much."
In her last moments, she spoke not of pain, nor the vast
incredulity of death,
but of love. That memory is better than a thousand prayers,
the depth of her love.

And I imagine in those images our friends bestow, there is
a certain love;
something so intense that they offer it to bring back health
and extend life:
see, here's a splinter of the true cross. Here's a bone of St.
Monica. Well,
a sliver the size of a dot anyway. And a drop of oil to be
rubbed on the diseased part,
a drop of water. Believe, not in the cross, the bone, the oil,
the water, the bead.
Believe in our friendship, our kinship. Hold my hand, the
sacred relics
at the center of our joined hands. Live.

Inner Child Press

News

We are so excited to announce the New and upcoming books of some of our Poetry Posse authors.

On the following pages we present to you ...

Jackie Davis Allen

Gail Weston Shazor

hülya n. yılmaz

Nizar Sartawi

Faleeha Hassan

Albert Carrasco

Caroline 'Ceri' Nazareno

Now Available at
www.innerchildpress.com

Dark Side
of the
Moon

Jackie Davis Allen

Now Available at

www.innerchildpress.com

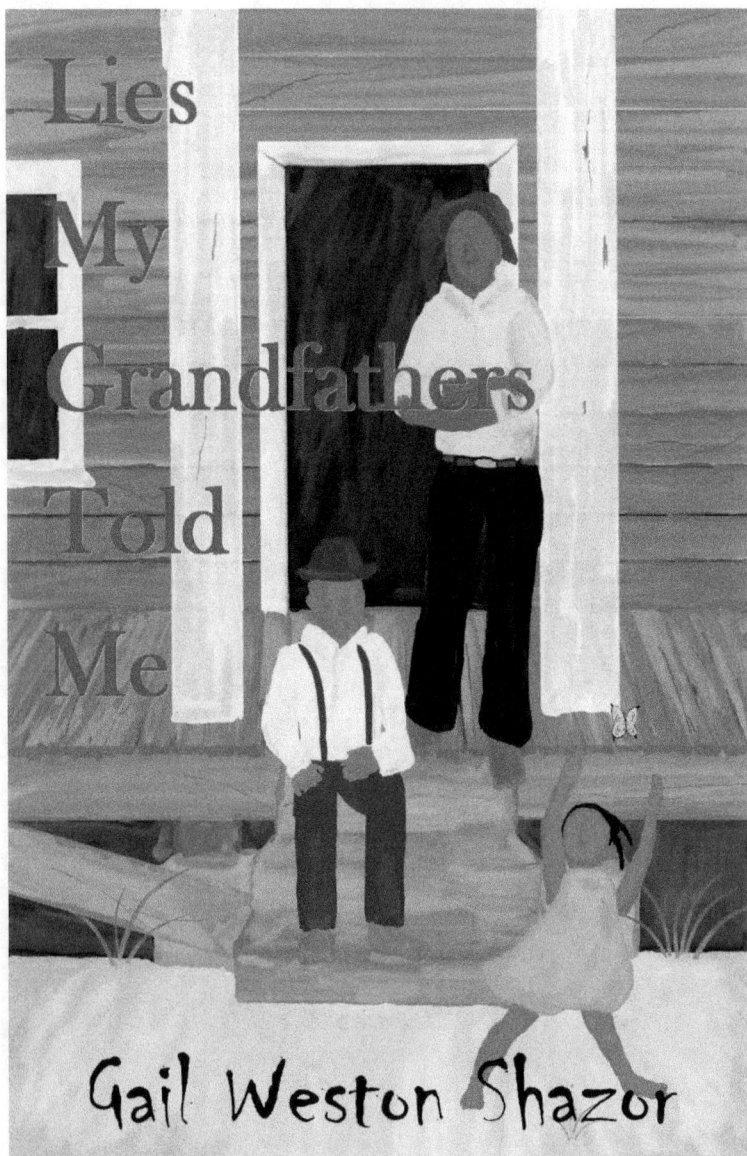

Lies My Grandfathers Told Me

Gail Weston Shazor

Now Available at
www.innerchildpress.com

Aflame

Memoirs in Verse

hülya n. yılmaz

Now Available at
www.innerchildpress.com

My Shadow

Nizar Sartawi

Now Available at
www.innerchildpress.com

Mass Graves

Faleeha Hassan

Coming Soon

Coming Soon

Other

Anthological

works from

Inner Child Press, ltd.

www.innerchildpress.com

Now Available

www.innerchildpress.com/janet-p-caldwell.php

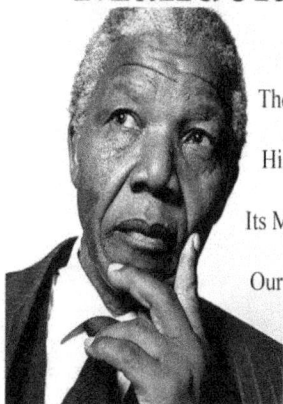

Mandela

The Man

His Life

Its Meaning

Our Words

Poetry . . . Commentary & Stories
The Anthological Writers

A GATHERING OF WORDS

POETRY & COMMENTARY
FOR
TRAYVON MARTIN

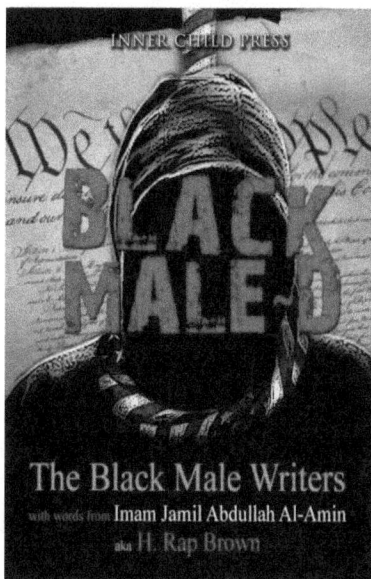

INNER CHILD PRESS

BLACK MALE-D

The Black Male Writers
with words from Imam Jamil Abdullah Al-Amin
aka H. Rap Brown

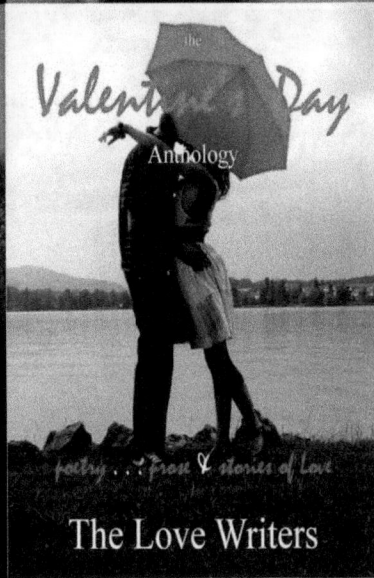

healing through words

Poetry ... Prose ... Prayer ... Stories

a
Poetically
Spoken
Anthology
volume I
Collector's Edition

The Poetry Posse
Presents

an anthology
of

Love

The Poetry Posse 2016

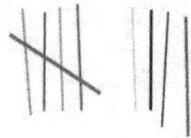

i
want my
PoEtRy
to . . .
a collection of the Voices of Many inspired by . . .
Monte Smith

a collection of the Voices of Many inspired by . . .
Monte Smith
i
want my
PoEtRy
to . . .
volume II

i
want my
PoEtRy
to . . . volume 3
a collection of the Voices of Many inspired by . . .
Monte Smith

11 Words
(9 lines . . .)
for those who are challenged
an anthology of Poetry inspired by . . .
Poetry Dancer

The Year of the Poet
January 2014

The Poetry Posse

Jamie Bond
Gail Weston Shazor
Albert 'Infinite' Carrasco
Siddartha Beth Pierce
Janet P. Caldwell
June 'Bugg' Barefield
Debbie M. Allen
Tony Henninger
Joe DaVerbal Minddancer
Robert Gibbons
Neetu Wali
Shareef Abdur-Rasheed
William S. Peters, Sr.

Carnation

Our January Feature
Terri L. Johnson

the Year of the Poet
February 2014

violets

The Poetry Posse
Jamie Bond
Gail Weston Shazor
Albert 'Infinite' Carrasco
Siddartha Beth Pierce
Janet P. Caldwell
June 'Bugg' Barefield
Debbie M. Allen
Tony Henninger
Joe DaVerbal Minddancer
Robert Gibbons
Neetu Wali
Shareef Abdur-Rasheed
William S. Peters, Sr.

Our February Features
Teresa E. Gallion & Robert Gibson

the Year of the Poet
March 2014

The Poetry Posse
Jamie Bond
Gail Weston Shazor
Albert 'Infinite' Carrasco
Siddartha Beth Pierce
Janet P. Caldwell
June 'Bugg' Barefield
Debbie M. Allen
Tony Henninger
Joe DaVerbal Minddancer
Robert Gibbons
Neetu Wali
Shareef Abdur-Rasheed
Kimberly Burnham
William S. Peters, Sr.

daffodil

Our March Featured Poets
Alicia C. Cooper & hülya yılmaz

the Year of the Poet
April 2014

The Poetry Posse
Jamie Bond
Gail Weston Shazor
Albert 'Infinite' Carrasco
Siddartha Beth Pierce
Janet P. Caldwell
June 'Bugg' Barefield
Debbie M. Allen
Tony Henninger
Joe DaVerbal Minddancer
Robert Gibbons
Neetu Wali
Shareef Abdur-Rasheed
Kimberly Burnham
William S. Peters, Sr.

Our April Featured Poets
Fahredin Shehu
Martina Reisz Newberry
Justin Blackburn
Monte Smith

Sweet Pea

celebrating international poetry month

the year of the poet
May 2014

May's Featured Poets
ReeCee
Joski the Poet
Shannon Stanton

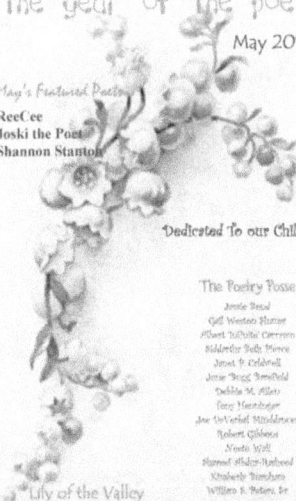

Dedicated To our Children

The Poetry Posse

Lily of the Valley

the Year of the Poet
June 2014

Love & Relationship

Rose

June's Featured Poets
Shantelle McLin
Jacqueline D. E. Kennedy
Abraham N. Benjamin

The Poetry Posse
Jamie Bond
Gail Weston Shazor
Albert 'Infinite' Carrasco
Siddartha Beth Pierce
Janet P. Caldwell
Junie 'Bugg' Barefield
Debbie M. Allen
Tony Henninger
Joe DaVerbal Minddancer
Robert Gibbons
Neetu Wali
Shareef Abdur-Rasheed
Kimberly Burnham
William S. Peters, Sr.

The Year of the Poet
July 2014

July Feature Poets
Christena A. V. Williams
Dr. John R. Strum
Rolade Otonrewaju Freedom

The Poetry Posse
Jamie Bond
Gail Weston Shazor

Lotus
Asian Flower of the Month

The Year of the Poet
August 2014

Gladiolus

The Poetry Posse
Jamie Bond
Gail Weston Shazor
Albert 'Infinite' Carrasco
Siddartha Beth Pierce
Janet P. Caldwell
Junie 'Bugg' Barefield
Debbie M. Allen
Tony Henninger
Joe DaVerbal Minddancer
Robert Gibbons
Neetu Wali
Shareef Abdur-Rasheed
Kimberly Burnham
William S. Peters, Sr.

August Feature Poets
Ann White * Rosalind Cherry * Shelia Jenkins

The Year of the Poet
September 2014

Aster   Morning-Glory

Wild Chaplet September Birth of Flower

September Feature Poets
Florence Malone • Keith Alan Hamilton

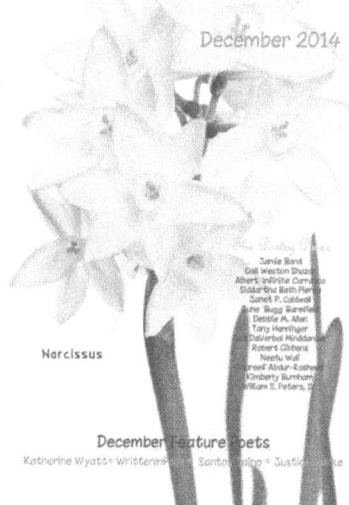

The Poetry Posse
Jamie Bond • Gail Weston Shazor • Albert 'Infinite' Carrasco • Siddartha Beth Pierce
Janet P. Caldwell • June 'Bugg' Barefield • Debbie M. Allen • Tony Henninger
Joe DaVerbal Minddancer • Robert Gibbons • Neetu Wali • Shareef Abdur-Rasheed
Kimberly Burnham • William S. Peters, Sr.

THE YEAR OF THE POET
October 2014

Red Poppy

The Poetry Posse
Jamie Bond • Gail Weston Shazor • Albert 'Infinite' Carrasco • Siddartha Beth Pierce
Janet P. Caldwell • June 'Bugg' Barefield • Debbie M. Allen • Tony Henninger
Joe DaVerbal Minddancer • Robert Gibbons • Neetu Wali • Shareef Abdur-Rasheed
Kimberly Burnham • William S. Peters, Sr.

October Feature Poets
Ceri Naz • Rajendra Padhi • Elizabeth Castillo

THE YEAR OF THE POET
November 2014

Chrysanthemum

The Poetry Posse
Jamie Bond • Gail Weston Shazor • Albert 'Infinite' Carrasco • Siddartha Beth Pierce
Janet P. Caldwell • June 'Bugg' Barefield • Debbie M. Allen • Tony Henninger
Joe DaVerbal Minddancer • Robert Gibbons • Neetu Wali • Shareef Abdur-Rasheed
Kimberly Burnham • William S. Peters, Sr.

November Feature Poets
Jocelyn Mosman • Jackie Allen • James Moore • Neville Hiatt

THE YEAR OF THE POET
December 2014

The Poetry Posse
Jamie Bond
Gail Weston Shazor
Albert 'Infinite' Carrasco
Siddartha Beth Pierce
Janet P. Caldwell
June 'Bugg' Barefield
Debbie M. Allen
Tony Henninger
DaVerbal Minddancer
Robert Gibbons
Neetu Wali
Shareef Abdur-Rasheed
Kimberly Burnham
William S. Peters, Sr.

Narcissus

December Feature Poets
Katherine Wyatt• Writtenin•••• Santos•••• • Justi•••••ke

THE YEAR OF THE POET II
January 2015

Garnet

The Poetry Posse

Jamie Bond
Gail Weston Shazor
Albert 'Infinite' Carrasco
Siddartha Beth Pierce
Janet P. Caldwell
Tony Henninger
Joe DaVerbal Minddancer
Robert Gibbons
Neetu Wali
Shareef Abdur – Rasheed
Kimberly Burnham
Ann White
Keith Alan Hamilton
Katherine Wyatt
Fahredin Shehu
Hülya N. Yılmaz
Teresa E. Gallion
Jackie Allen
William S. Peters, Sr.

January Feature Poets
Bismay Mohanti * Jen Walls * Eric Judah

THE YEAR OF THE POET ii
February 2015

Amethyst

THE POETRY POSSE
Jamie Bond
Gail Weston Shazor
Albert 'Infinite' Carrasco
Siddartha Beth Pierce
Janet P. Caldwell
Tony Henninger
Joe DaVerbal Minddancer
Robert Gibbons
Neetu Wali
Shareef Abdur – Rasheed
Kimberly Burnham
Ann White
Keith Alan Hamilton
Katherine Wyatt
Fahredin Shehu
Hülya N. Yılmaz
Teresa E. Gallion
Jackie Allen
William S. Peters, Sr.

FEBRUARY FEATURE POETS
Iram Fatima * Bob McNeil * Kerstin Centervall

The Year of the Poet II
March 2015

Our Featured Poets
Heung Sook * Anthony Arnold * Alicia Poland

Bloodstone

The Poetry Posse 2015
Jamie Bond * Gail Weston Shazor * Albert 'Infinite' Carrasco
Siddartha Beth Pierce * Janet P. Caldwell * Tony Henninger
Joe DaVerbal Minddancer * Neetu Wali * Shareef Abdur – Rasheed
Kimberly Burnham * Ann White * Keith Alan Hamilton
Katherine Wyatt * Fahredin Shehu * Hülya N. Yılmaz
Teresa E. Gallion * Jackie Allen * William S. Peters, Sr.

The Year of the Poet II
April 2015

Celebrating International Poetry Month

Our Featured Poets
Raja Williams * Dennis Ferado * Laure Charazac

Diamonds

The Poetry Posse 2015
Jamie Bond * Gail Weston Shazor * Albert 'Infinite' Carrasco
Siddartha Beth Pierce * Janet P. Caldwell * Tony Henninger
Joe DaVerbal Minddancer * Neetu Wali * Shareef Abdur – Rasheed
Kimberly Burnham * Ann White * Keith Alan Hamilton
Katherine Wyatt * Fahredin Shehu * Hülya N. Yılmaz
Teresa E. Gallion * Jackie Allen * William S. Peters, Sr.

The Year of the Poet II
May 2015

May's Featured Poets

Geri Algeri
Akin Mosi Chinneux
Anna Jakubcza

Emeralds

The Poetry Posse 2015

Jamie Bond * Gail Weston Shazor * Albert 'Infinite' Carrasco
Siddartha Beth Pierce * Janet P. Caldwell * Tony Henninger
Joe DaVerbal Minddancer * Neetu Wali * Shareef Abdur – Rasheed
Kimberly Burnham * Ann White * Keith Alan Hamilton
Katherine Wyatt * Fahredin Shehu * Hülya N. Yılmaz
Teresa E. Gallion * Jackie Allen * William S. Peters, Sr.

The Year of the Poet II
June 2015

June's Featured Poets

Anahit Arustamyan * Yvette D. Murrell * Regina A. Walker

Pearl

The Poetry Posse 2015

Jamie Bond * Gail Weston Shazor * Albert 'Infinite' Carrasco
Siddartha Beth Pierce * Janet P. Caldwell * Tony Henninger
Joe DaVerbal Minddancer * Neetu Wali * Shareef Abdur – Rasheed
Kimberly Burnham * Ann White * Keith Alan Hamilton
Katherine Wyatt * Fahredin Shehu * Hülya N. Yılmaz
Teresa E. Gallion * Jackie Allen * William S. Peters, Sr

The Year of the Poet II
July 2015

The Featured Poets for July 2015
Abhik Shome * Christina Neal * Robert Neal

Rubies

The Poetry Posse 2015

Jamie Bond * Gail Weston Shazor * Albert 'Infinite' Carrasco
Siddartha Beth Pierce * Janet P. Caldwell * Tony Henninger
Joe DaVerbal Minddancer * Neetu Wali * Shareef Abdur – Rasheed
Kimberly Burnham * Ann White * Keith Alan Hamilton
Katherine Wyatt * Fahredin Shehu * Hülya N. Yılmaz
Teresa E. Gallion * Jackie Allen * William S. Peters, Sr.

The Year of the Poet II
August 2015

Peridot

Featured Poets
Gayle Howell
Ann Chalasz
Christopher Schultz

The Poetry Posse 2015

Jamie Bond * Gail Weston Shazor * Albert 'Infinite' Carrasco
Siddartha Beth Pierce * Janet P. Caldwell * Tony Henninger
Joe DaVerbal Minddancer * Neetu Wali * Shareef Abdur – Rasheed
Kimberly Burnham * Ann White * Keith Alan Hamilton
Katherine Wyatt * Fahredin Shehu * Hülya N. Yılmaz
Teresa E. Gallion * Jackie Allen * William S. Peters, Sr

The Year of the Poet II
September 2015

Featured Poets
Alfreda Ghee · Lonneice Weeks Badley · Demetrios Trifiatis

Sapphires

The Poetry Posse 2015

Jamie Bond * Gail Weston Shazor * Albert 'Infinite' Carrasco
Siddartha Beth Pierce * Janet P. Caldwell * Tony Henninger
Joe DaVerbal Minddancer * Neetu Wali * Shareef Abdur – Rasheed
Kimberly Burnham * Ann White * Keith Alan Hamilton
Katherine Wyatt * Fahredin Shehu * Hülya N. Yılmaz
Teresa E. Gallion * Jackie Allen * William S. Peters, Sr.

The Year of the Poet II
October 2015

Featured Poets
Monte Smith * Laura J. Wolfe * William Washington

Opal

The Poetry Posse 2015

Jamie Bond * Gail Weston Shazor * Albert 'Infinite' Carrasco
Siddartha Beth Pierce * Janet P. Caldwell * Tony Henninger
Joe DaVerbal Minddancer * Neetu Wali * Shareef Abdur – Rasheed
Kimberly Burnham * Ann White * Keith Alan Hamilton
Katherine Wyatt * Fahredin Shehu * Hülya N. Yılmaz
Teresa E. Gallion * Jackie Allen * William S. Peters, Sr.

The Year of the Poet II
November 2015

Featured Poets
Alan W. Jankowski
Bismay Mohanty
James Moore

Topaz

The Poetry Posse 2015

Jamie Bond * Gail Weston Shazor * Albert 'Infinite' Carrasco
Siddartha Beth Pierce * Janet P. Caldwell * Tony Henninger
Joe DaVerbal Minddancer * Neetu Wali * Shareef Abdur – Rasheed
Kimberly Burnham * Ann White * Keith Alan Hamilton
Katherine Wyatt * Fahredin Shehu * Hülya N. Yılmaz
Teresa E. Gallion * Jackie Allen * William S. Peters, Sr.

The Year of the Poet II
December 2015

Featured Poets
Kerione Bryan * Michelle Joan Barulich * Neville Hiatt

Turquoise

The Poetry Posse 2015

Jamie Bond * Gail Weston Shazor * Albert 'Infinite' Carrasco
Siddartha Beth Pierce * Janet P. Caldwell * Tony Henninger
Joe DaVerbal Minddancer * Neetu Wali * Shareef Abdur – Rasheed
Kimberly Burnham * Ann White * Keith Alan Hamilton
Katherine Wyatt * Fahredin Shehu * Hülya N. Yılmaz
Teresa E. Gallion * Jackie Allen * William S. Peters, Sr.

164

The Year of the Poet III
January 2016

Featured Poets

Lana Joseph * Atom Cyrus Rush * Christena Williams

Dark-eyed Junco

The Poetry Posse 2016

Gail Weston Shazor * Anne Jakubczak Vel Ratty Adalan * Ynes J. White
Eferedo Shebu * Hrishikesh Padhye * Janet P. Caldwell
Joe 'DaVerbal' Minddancer * Shareef Abdur - Rasheed
Albert Carrasco * Kimberly Burnham * Keith Alan Hamilton
Hülya N. Yılmaz * Demetrios Trifiatis * Alan W. Jankowski
Teresa E. Gallion * Jackie Davis Allen * William S. Peters, Sr.

The Year of the Poet III
February 2016

Featured Poets
Anthony Arnold
Anna Chalasz
Andre Hawthorne

Puffin

The Poetry Posse 2016

Gail Weston Shazor * Joe DaVerbal Minddancer * Efereda Ghee
Efereda Shebu * Hrishikesh Padhye * Janet P. Caldwell
Anne Jakubczak Vel Ratty Adalan * Shareef Abdur - Rasheed
Albert Carrasco * Kimberly Burnham * Ynes J. White
Hülya N. Yılmaz * Demetrios Trifiatis * Alan W. Jankowski
Teresa E. Gallion * Jackie Davis Allen * William S. Peters, Sr.

The Year of the Poet
March 2016

Featured Poets

Jeton Kelmendi   Nizar Sartawi   Sami Muhanna

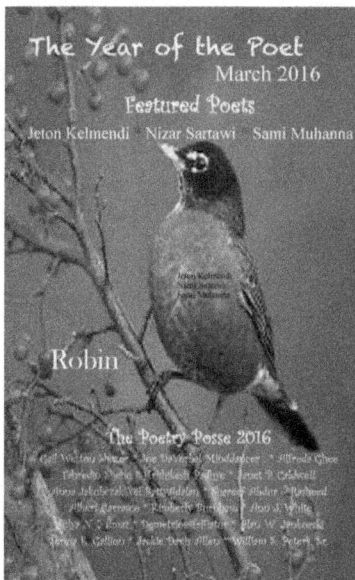

Robin

The Poetry Posse 2016

Gail Weston Shazor * Joe DaVerbal Minddancer * Efereda Ghee
Efereda Shebu * Hrishikesh Padhye * Janet P. Caldwell
Anne Jakubczak Vel Ratty Adalan * Shareef Abdur - Rasheed
Albert Carrasco * Kimberly Burnham * Ynes J. White
Hülya N. Yılmaz * Demetrios Trifiatis * Alan W. Jankowski
Teresa E. Gallion * Jackie Davis Allen * William S. Peters, Sr.

The Year of the Poet III

Featured Poets

Ali Abdolrezaei

Anna Chalasz

Agim Vinca

Ceri Naz

Black Capped Chickadee

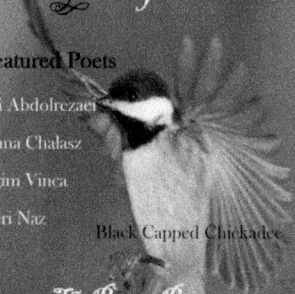

The Poetry Posse 2016

Gail Weston Shazor * Joe DaVerbal Minddancer * Afresh Ghee
Fahredin Shehu * Hrishikesh Padhye * Janet P. Caldwell
Anna Jakubczak Vel Ratty Adalan * Shareef Abdur - Rasheed
Albert Carrasco * Kimberly Burnham * Ynes J. White
Hülya N. Yılmaz * Demetrios Trifiatis * Alan W. Jankowski
Teresa E. Gallion * Jackie Davis Allen * William S. Peters, Sr.

celebrating international poetry month

The Year of the Poet
May 2016

Bob Strum
Barbara Allan
D.L. Davis

Oriole

The Year of the Poet III
June 2016

Featured Poets

Qibrije Demiri- Frangu
Naime Beqiraj
Faleeha Hassan
Bedri Zyberaj

Black Necked Stilt

The Poetry Posse 2016

The Year of the Poet
July 2016

Iram Fatima 'Ashi'
Langley Shazor
Jody Doty
Emilia T. Davis

Indigo Bunting

The Poetry Posse 2016

The Year of the Poet III
August 2016

Featured Poets

Anita Dash
Irena Jovanovic
Malgorzata Gouluda

Painted Bunting

The Poetry Posse 2016

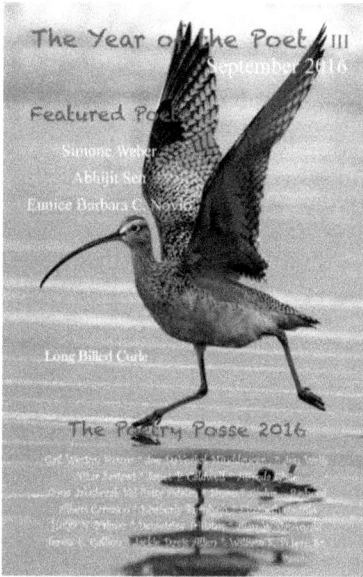

The Year of the Poet III
September 2016

Featured Poets

Simone Weber
Abhijit Sen
Eunice Barbara C. Novio

Long Billed Curle

The Poetry Posse 2016

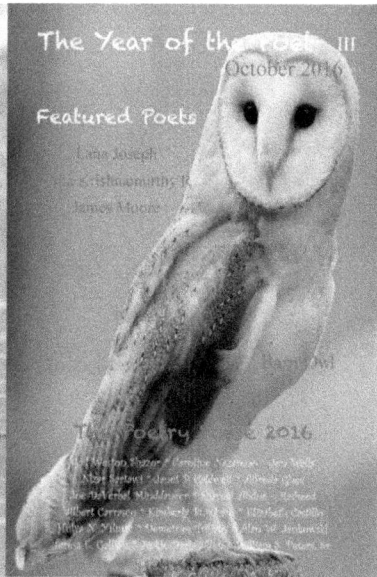

The Year of the Poet III
October 2016

Featured Poets

Lina Joseph
S. Ishmuamith;
James Moore

The Poetry Posse 2016

The Year of the Poet III
November 2016

Featured Poets

Rosemary Burns
Robin Ouzman Hislop
Lonneice Weeks-Badler

Northern Cardinal

The Poetry Posse 2016

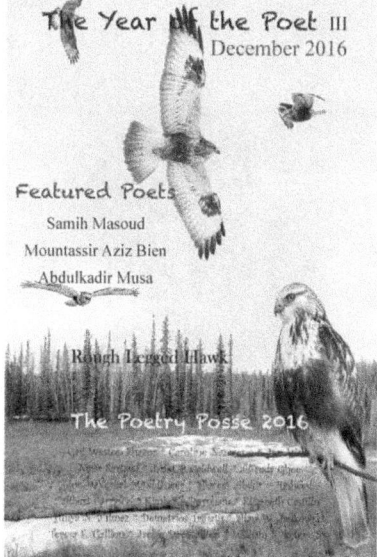

The Year of the Poet III
December 2016

Featured Poets

Samih Masoud
Mountassir Aziz Bien
Abdulkadir Musa

Rough Legged Hawk

The Poetry Posse 2016

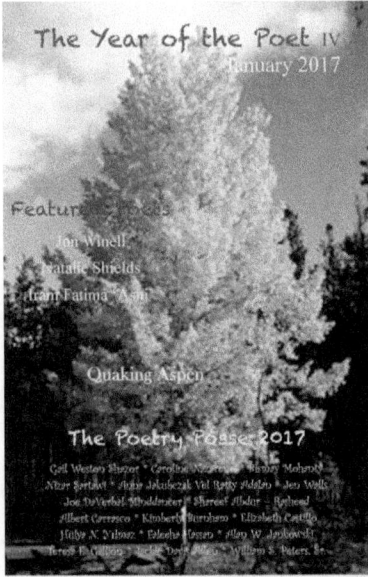

The Year of the Poet IV
January 2017

Featured Poets
Jon Winell
Natalie Shields
Grant Fatima 'Asai

Quaking Aspen

The Poetry Posse 2017

Gail Weston Shazor * Caroline Nazareno * Panay Mohanty
Nizar Sartawi * Anne Jakubczak Vel Ratty Adalan * Jen Wells
Joe DaVerbal Minddancer * Shireef Abdur – Rasheed
Albert Carrasco * Kimberly Burnham * Elizabeth Castillo
Hülya N. Yılmaz * Teleeho Hassan * Alan W. Jankowski
Teresa E. Gallion * Jackie Davis Allen * William S. Peters, Sr.

The Year of the Poet IV
February 2017

Featured Poets
Lin Ross
Soukaina Fatih
Arwer Gitani

Witch Hazel

The Poetry Posse 2017

Gail Weston Shazor * Caroline Nazareno * Panay Mohanty
Nizar Sartawi * Anne Jakubczak Vel Ratty Adalan * Jen Wells
Joe DaVerbal Minddancer * Shireef Abdur – Rasheed
Albert Carrasco * Kimberly Burnham * Elizabeth Castillo
Hülya N. Yılmaz * Teleeho Hassan * Alan W. Jankowski
Teresa E. Gallion * Jackie Davis Allen * William S. Peters, Sr.

The Year of the Poet IV
March 2017

Featured Poets
Tremell Stevens
Francisca Ricinski
Jamil Abu Shaih

The Eastern Redbud

The Poetry Posse 2017

Gail Weston Shazor * Caroline Nazareno * Panay Mohanty
Teresa E. Gallion * Anne Jakubczak Vel Ratty Adalan
Joe DaVerbal Minddancer * Shireef Abdur – Rasheed
Albert Carrasco * Kimberly Burnham * Elizabeth Castillo
Hülya N. Yılmaz * Teleeho Hassan * Jackie Davis Allen
Jen Wells * Nizar Sartawi * * William S. Peters, Sr.

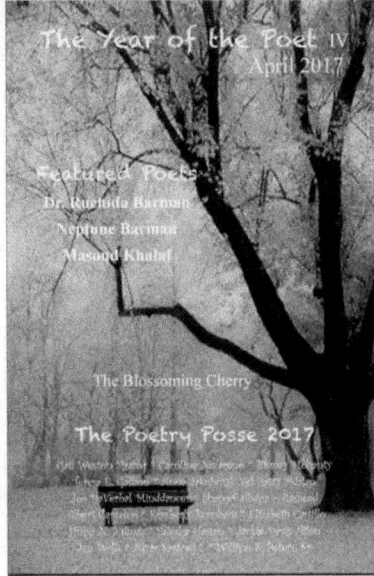

The Year of the Poet IV
April 2017

Featured Poets
Dr. Ruchida Barman
Neptune Barman
Masood Khalaf

The Blossoming Cherry

The Poetry Posse 2017

Gail Weston Shazor * Caroline Nazareno * Panay Mohanty
Nizar Sartawi * Anne Jakubczak Vel Ratty Adalan * Jen Wells
Joe DaVerbal Minddancer * Shireef Abdur – Rasheed
Albert Carrasco * Kimberly Burnham * Elizabeth Castillo
Hülya N. Yılmaz * Teleeho Hassan * Jackie Davis Allen
Jen Wells * Nizar Sartawi * * William S. Peters, Sr.

The Year of the Poet IV
May 2017

The Flowering Dogwood Tree

Featured Poets
Kallisa Powell
Alicja Maria Kuberska
Fethi Sassi

The Poetry Posse 2017

The Year of the Poet IV
June 2017

Featured Poets
Eliza Segiet
Tzu-Min Tsai
Abdulla Issa

The Linden Tree

The Poetry Posse 2017

The Year of the Poet IV
July 2017

Featured Poets
Anca Mihaela Bruma
Ibaa Ismail
Zvonko Taneski

The Oak Moon

The Poetry Posse 2017

The Year of the Poet IV
August 2017

Featured Poets
Jonathan Aquino
Kitty Hsu
Langley Shazor

The Hazelnut Tree

The Poetry Posse 2017

and there is much, much more !

visit . . .

http://www.innerchildpress.com
/anthologies-sales-special.php

Also check out our Authors and
all the wonderful Books
Available at :

http://www.innerchildpress.com
/the-book-store.php

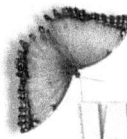

World Healing
World Peace

support

www.worldhealingworldpeacepoetry.com

Now Available

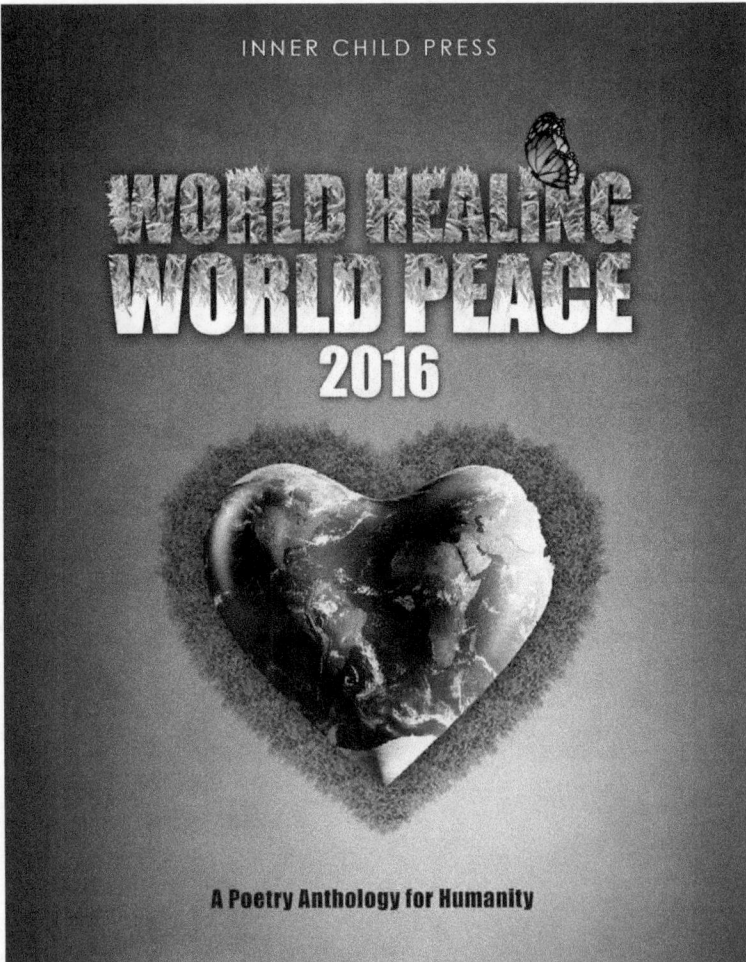

INNER CHILD PRESS

WORLD HEALING WORLD PEACE 2016

A Poetry Anthology for Humanity

www.worldhealingworldpeacepoetry.com

This Anthological Publication
is underwritten solely by

Inner Child Press

Inner Child Press is a Publishing Company
Founded and Operated by Writers. Our personal
publishing experiences provides us an intimate
understanding of the sometimes daunting
challenges Writers, New and Seasoned may face in
the Business of Publishing and Marketing their
Creative "Written Work".

For more Information

Inner Child Press

www.innerchildpress.com

Inner Child PRESS°

Let Us Share
Our *Magic* With *You*

www.innerchildpress.com

~ *fini* ~

174

174

www.ingramcontent.com/pod-product-compliance
Lightning Source LLC
LaVergne TN
LVHW051053080426
835508LV00019B/1849